SPECTRAL PEGASUS / DARK MOVEMENTS

Poems by Jeffery Beam
Paintings by Clive Hicks-Jenkins

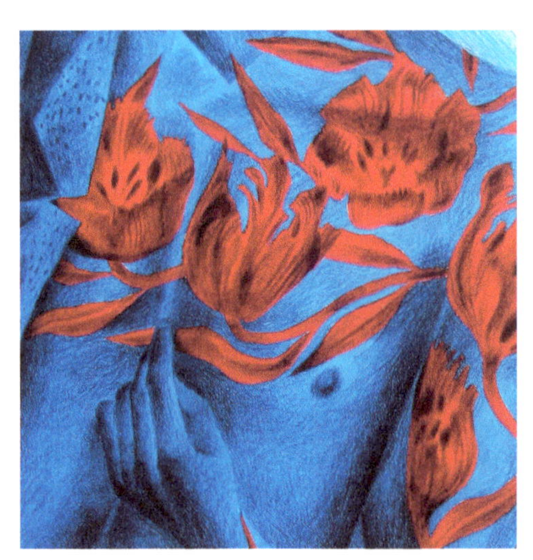

With gratitude to Clive for sharing his Hero's journey.
With love to Stanley for his patience and encouragement.

Additional thanks to Mary-Ann Constantine, Hubert Dean (Snow Hill Music),
Mark Kuniya (Country Valley Press), Maria Maestre, Jordan Morley,
Sarah Parvin (The Curious One), Claire Pickard, Mary Rocap,
F.J. Ventre (Tadpole Designs), Peter Wakelin, and Marly Youmans
for their inspiration and comradery on the journey.

My gratitude to Joseph Bathanti, Lindsay Clarke, Damian Walford Davies, Kent Johnson,
Susan Rowland, and the Joseph Campbell Foundation for their hearings and sayings.

In memory of my beloved sister-in-law and friend Patricia Finch who from
Back of Beyond generously helped fund the CD and my new website.
May she read and hear in Peace and Elysian Gladness.

To my publishers: My eternal indebtedness, thus Everything and All, to J.C. Mlozanowski for her
patience, diligence, skill, and sympathetically exceptional design. And to Meg Cowen, my
appreciation for her early contributions to the publishing project and for the Kin Press imprint.

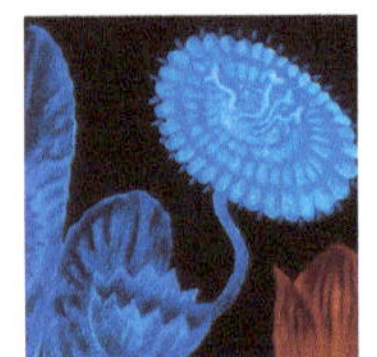 LET US begin by acknowledging that we are mysterious creatures inhabiting a mysterious world whose nature we do not understand, and where, if we are honest with ourselves, we will admit that, apart from the inevitability of death, there is nothing fundamental that we know for certain. Despite our best convictions, we do not know who we are, we don't know why we are here or what will become of us. This is, and has always been, the radical uncertainty of the human condition. Out of that uncertainty arise all the stories and stratagems by which we strive as best we can to connive at life and shape it to our purposes, to seek to make a go of things, to try to become what we believe ourselves to be, while attempting at the same time to make sense of the others around us who are caught up in the same marvelous and fateful game. Thus it can be seen that, whether we are conscious of it or not, our powerful culture is now far advanced on such a Hades Journey. But as long as we continue to devolve the suffering on those less fortunate than ourselves, or to look for solutions in mere amelioration of the attitudes that precipitated the current planetary crisis, we will get lost on the journey and fall asleep in our own dark shadows. Yet to push on through will make severe demands on us. It will require a willingness to subordinate the ego's narrow ambitions to the wider claims of the compassionate imagination. It will demand more serious respect for those feminine—or lunar—values which, because they are not easily quantified or controlled, have been too long demeaned and neglected in our culture. It will involve a revaluation of the ancient wisdom of the ancestors, not only as found in surviving texts, but as a part of our genetic structure—the dead ancestors alive inside each of us, speaking through our dreams and genes. Lastly, and most comprehensively, it will require an honest responsiveness to the intelligence of the earth itself, of which each one of us is a living filament. In short, only by undergoing such ordeals of self-divestiture will our Hades Journey be completed. The demands it makes will not easily be answered. But without a willing acceptance of its claims on us we may live and die in ignorance of who we truly are.

—Lindsay Clarke, *The Water Theatre*

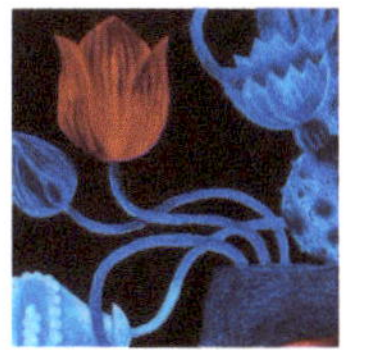IT IS the business of mythology proper, and of the fairy tale, to reveal the specific dangers and techniques of the dark interior way from tragedy to comedy. Hence the incidents are fantastic and "unreal": they represent psychological, not physical, triumphs. Even when the legend is of an actual historical personage, the deeds of victory are rendered, not in lifelike, but in dreamlike figurations; for the point is not that such-and-such could be done on earth, this other, more important, primary thing had to be brought to pass within the labyrinth that we all know and visit in our dreams. The passage of the mythological hero may be over-ground, incidentally; fundamentally it is inward—into depths where obscure resistances are overcome, and long lost, forgotten powers are revivified, to be made available for the transfiguration of the world. This deed accomplished, life no longer suffers hopelessly under the terrible mutilations of ubiquitous disaster, battered by time, hideous throughout space; but with its horror visible still, its cries of anguish still tumultuous, it becomes penetrated by an all-suffusing, all-sustaining love, and a knowledge of its own unconquered power. Something of the light that blazes invisible within the abysses of its normally opaque materiality breaks forth, with an increasing uproar. The dreadful mutilations are then seen as shadows, only, of an immanent, imperishable eternity; time yields to glory; and the world sings with the prodigious, angelic, but perhaps finally monotonous, siren music of the spheres. Like happy families, the myths and the worlds redeemed are all alike… A hero ventures forth from the world of common day into a region of supernatural wonder: fabulous forces are there encountered and a decisive victory is won: the hero comes back from this mysterious adventure with the power to bestow boons on his fellow man.

—Joseph Campbell, from The Hero with a Thousand Faces

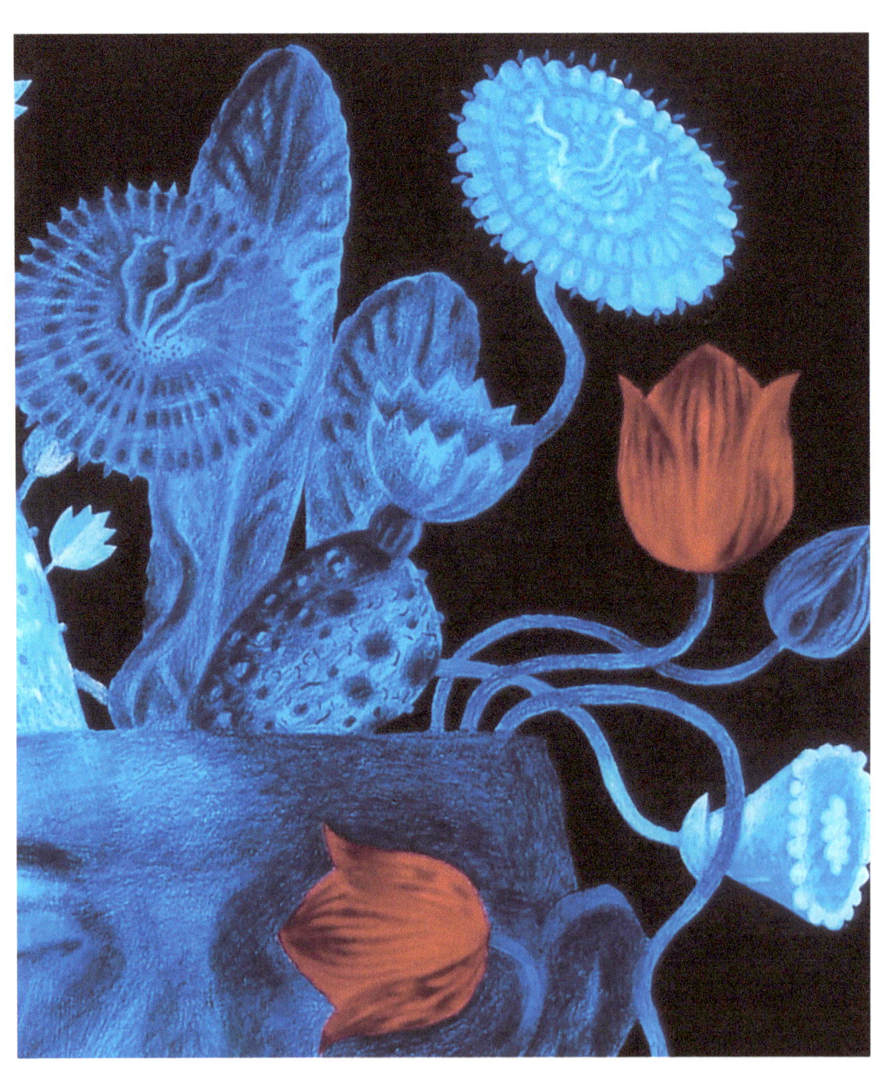

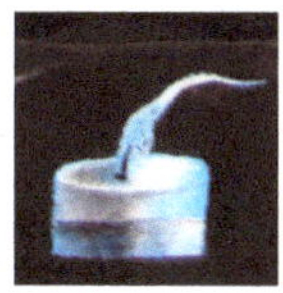 THESE POEMS were written in collaboration with Welsh painter Clive Hicks-Jenkins as he created his sequence of paintings *Dark Movements* leading to an exhibition at the Aberystwyth Arts Centre, Wales, June 10 – July 25, 2015.

In *Dark Movements* Hicks-Jenkins returned to the territory of his 2000-2001 series titled *The Mare's Tale*. To view those paintings: www.hicks-jenkins.com/new-gallery-1. Fifteen years brought about changes in his responses to his late father's recollections of a childhood run-in with the Mari Lwyd. The Mari Lwyd or "grey mare," a Welsh mid-winter tradition, has been a key influence in his work. The exhibition and series of events around it included a multi-media presentation of works inspired by the story. My poems were written in our white heat of January to June 2015 as Clive created the Jordan maquette, the Dark Movements Theater, and, ultimately, the paintings. I aimed to write a poem for each painting, but as Clive blogged and Facebooked about the progress of creation, and he and I, and Sarah Parvin, Jordan Morley, blog reader Maria Maestre, and my longtime friend (and friend of Clive's) novelist Marly Youmans corresponded with each other I was sometimes inspired to write additional poems. In this script, I added six "painting process" poems for images other than the ten final paintings, and I've even included one poem inspired by an image (Red Halter, 2001) from the original *The Mare's Tale* paintings. Three "painting process" poems, written in a different style, I have chosen to leave out of this script. The additional poems are background music to his lively living visual telling.

Because the folklore of the Mari Lwyd is relatively unknown outside of Welsh or British folklore studies, we have included a new essay, which was written by the art blogger and social media influencer, Sarah Parvin of The Curious One. She explores the relationship of the poems to the painting sequence, to the myth, and the poet's collaboration with Clive Hicks-Jenkins. Two short review essays, written by Mary-Ann Constantine and Claire Pickard and published in the Welsh press during the time of the exhibition, are also re-published at the book's end.

A selection from this book was published in a limited edition chapbook by Country Valley Press in 2017.

All images © 2015 Clive Hicks-Jenkins
"I Dreamed a Dream" © 2018 Sarah Parvin
Spectral Pegasus / Dark Movements poems and music © 2018 Jeffery Beam
"*Dark Movements*" essay © 2015 Mary-Ann Constantine, reprinted with permission
      from *Planet Magazine*
"A Note on Clive Hicks-Jenkins' *Dark Movements*" essay © 2015 Claire Pickard, reprinted
      with permission from *The New Welsh Review* blog
Quote from Lindsay Clarke's *The Water Theatre*, copyright © 2010, used with
      Permission, United Agents LLP on behalf of Lindsay Clarke
Quote from Joseph Campbell's *The Hero with a Thousand Faces*, copyright © Joseph
      Campbell Foundation (cf.org) 2008, used with permission

A limited edition CD of the poems and songs is available for $2.50 shipping and handling (500 copies, first come, first served). Inquires to the author through his website [see bio]. MP3 performance files can be heard on the poet's website. All poems and a "sung poem" are performed by the poet, and the poem/ballad "Pale Horse" is sung by the poet with accompaniment by singer and musician Mary Rocap. Recorded live at the studios of Snow Hill Music, Hillsborough, North Carolina, Summer 2018.

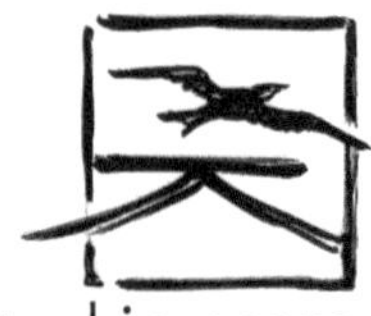

Published 2019 by kin press

PO Box 682, Higganum, CT 06441
ISBN 978-0-9989293-1-6

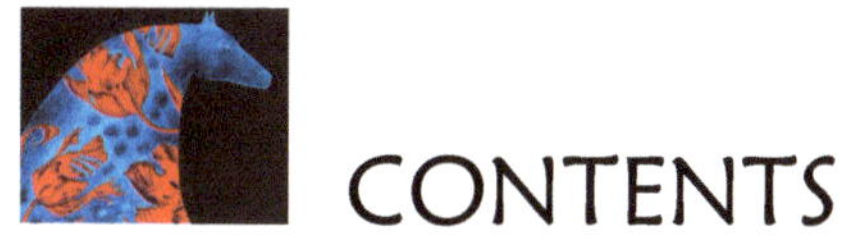

CONTENTS

*These paintings are in Clive's painting sequence *Dark Movements*. The painting *Red Halter* from Clive's *The Mare's Tale* accompanies the poem "Region of Shrouds."

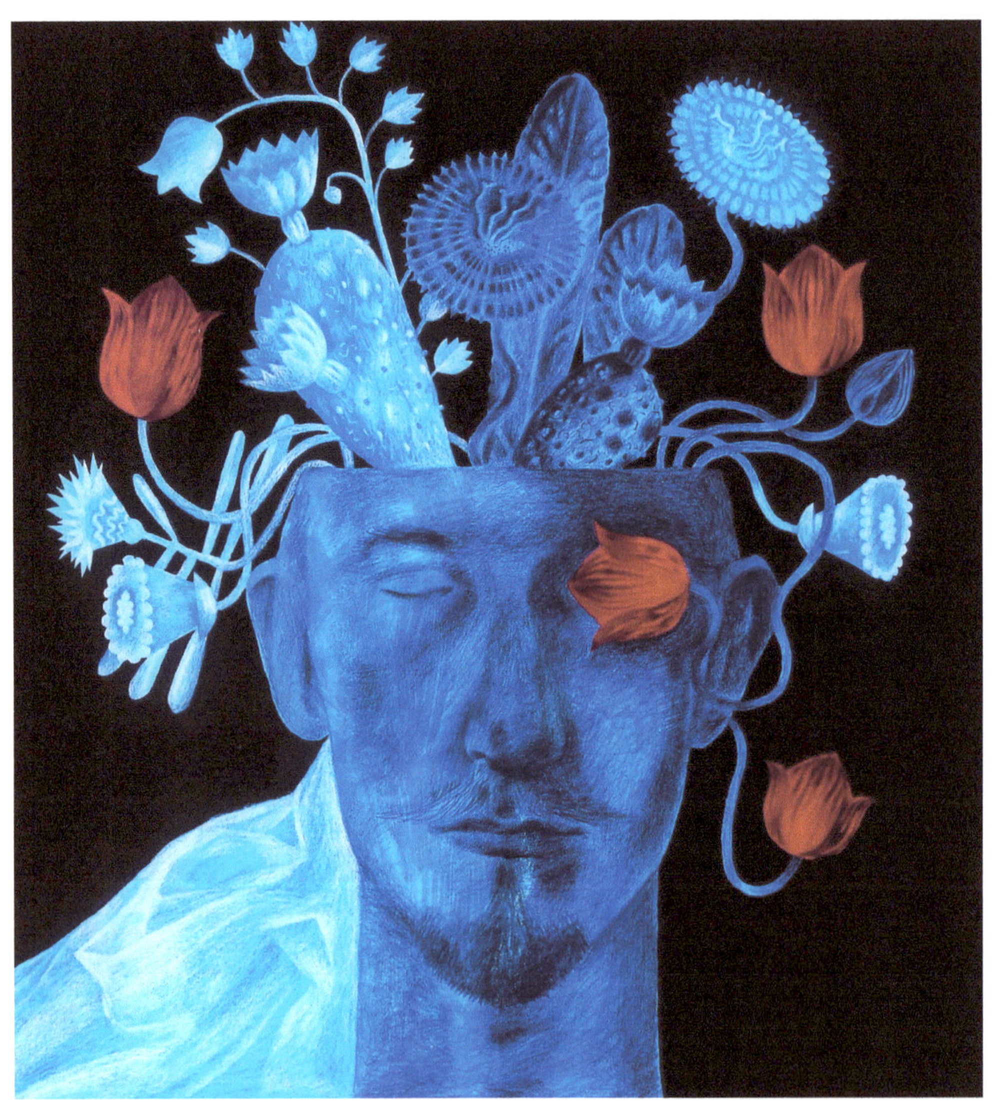

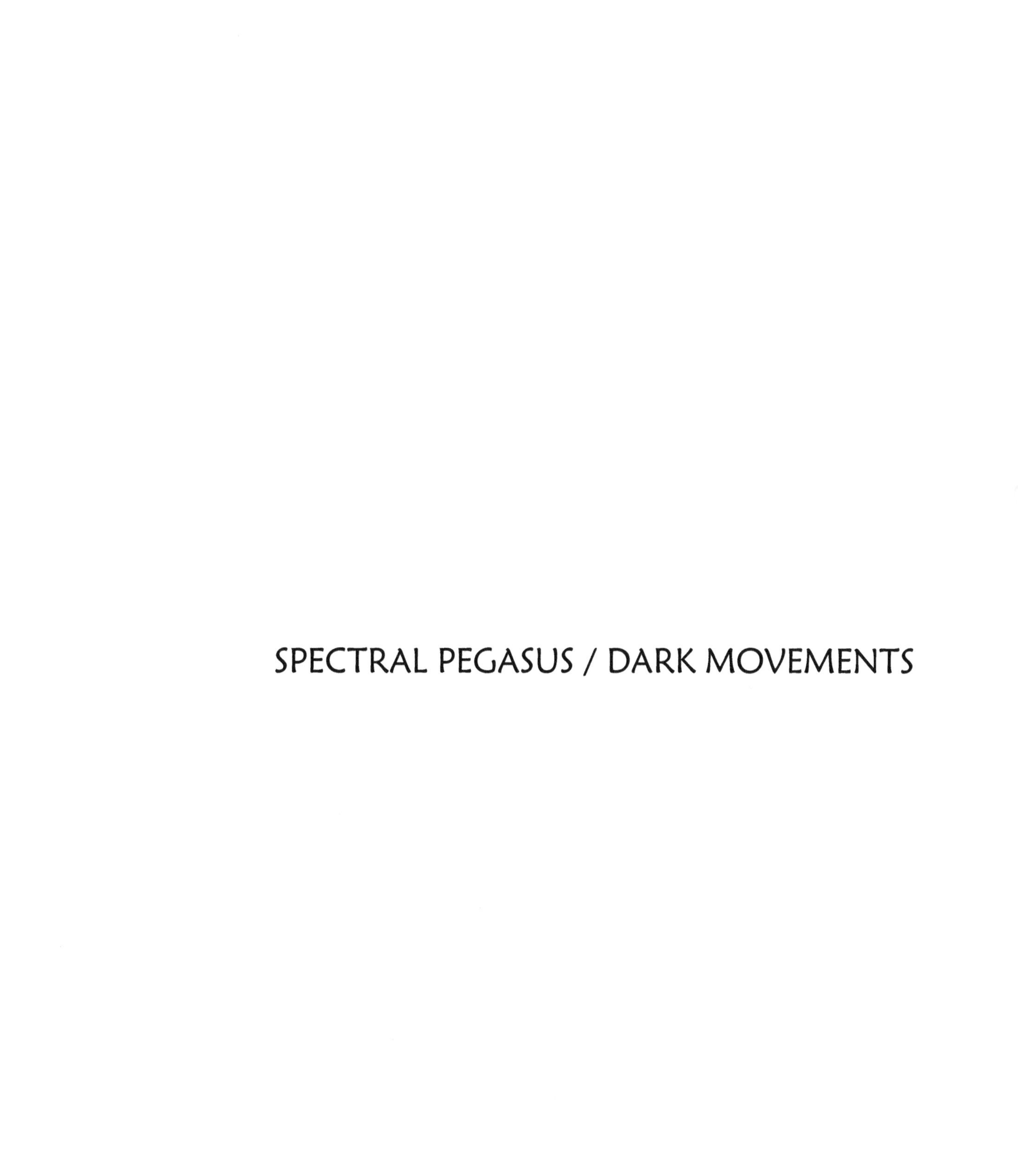

SPECTRAL PEGASUS / DARK MOVEMENTS

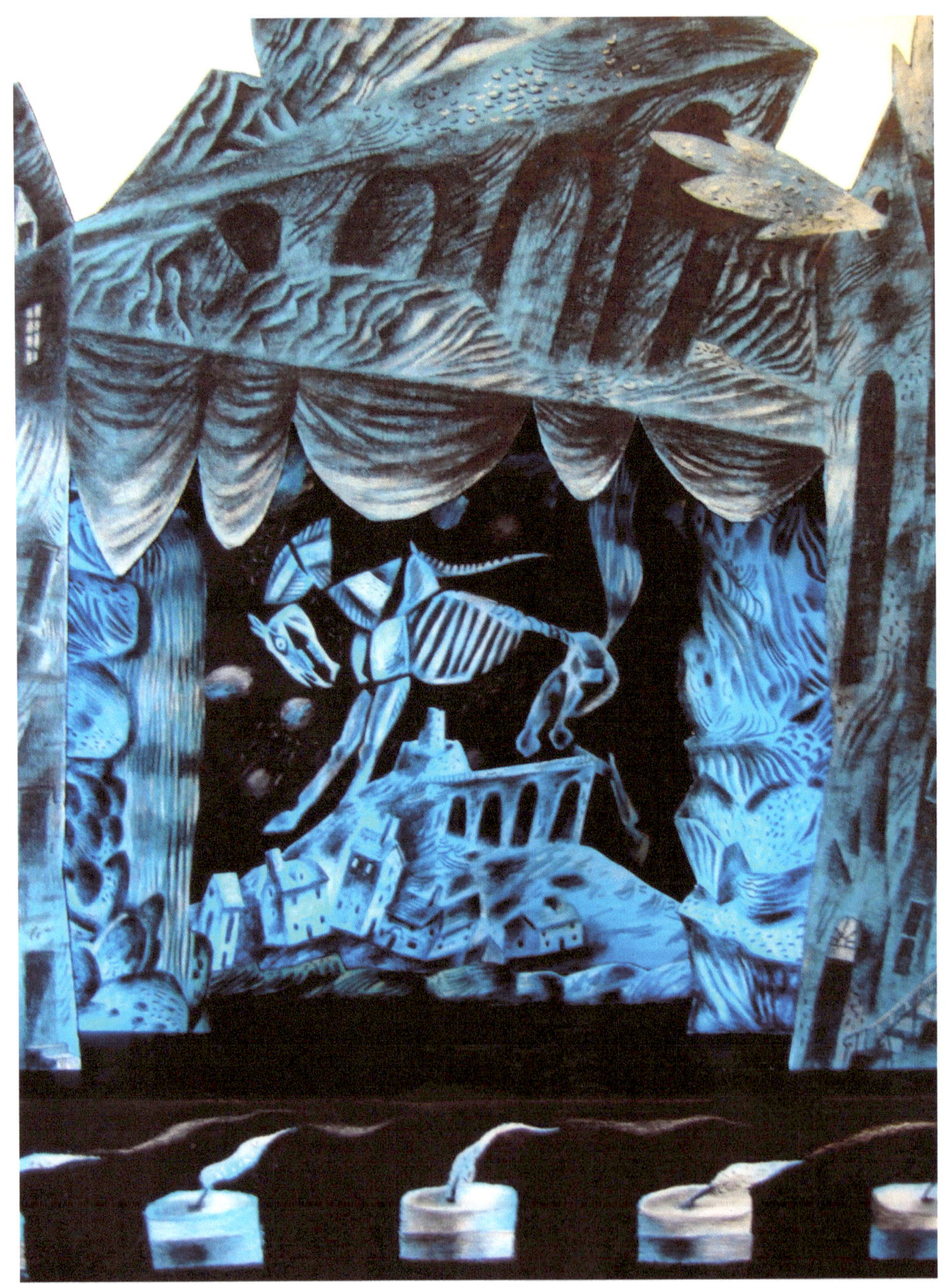

SPECTRAL PEGASUS

When Death came to me with four legs
I rode that Night Mare
White Apocalypse from the White Vale
She blazed blue

When She came to me with two I said
Walk with me beside me arm-in-arm
Let's watch the twilight tower lurch into sapphire
The tower from which I let
down my hair a mane of trouble
and silk

Mirror Horse of Heaven Haunt of Unseen Realms

The dead have died a thousand times
for they have died in me
I climb the signal tower each time I bend my knee
Across the rugged fells a silver bone bag a white shag
A man-pole shivering into ribbons
Arterial wince tributarial quake

Mirror Horse of Heaven Haunt of Unseen Realms

Ride me you'll not break my spirit
Jockey me into other eternities
Gallop me into entreating sleet
Veil your wings I know they are there

I feel their cold flapping in the black-blue dank
I feel their waterfall in my belly a cliff grasped in my hand
They throb and scorch cold fire cold flame blue flame

Mirror Horse of Heaven Haunt of Unseen Realms

When you come to me with two legs
You menace me into Salvation
Rock me nighttime sleeptime into delirious night
Delicious delirium delicious walk

Mirror Horse of Heaven Haunt of Unseen Realms

O rough and shuffling Thing merge your corrupting
wings into my ache
Wake me to your cove
Raise me to your White Vale White Village
Night Walk on four legs

I eat the Night I
welcome it

Mirror Horse of Heaven Haunt of Unseen Realms

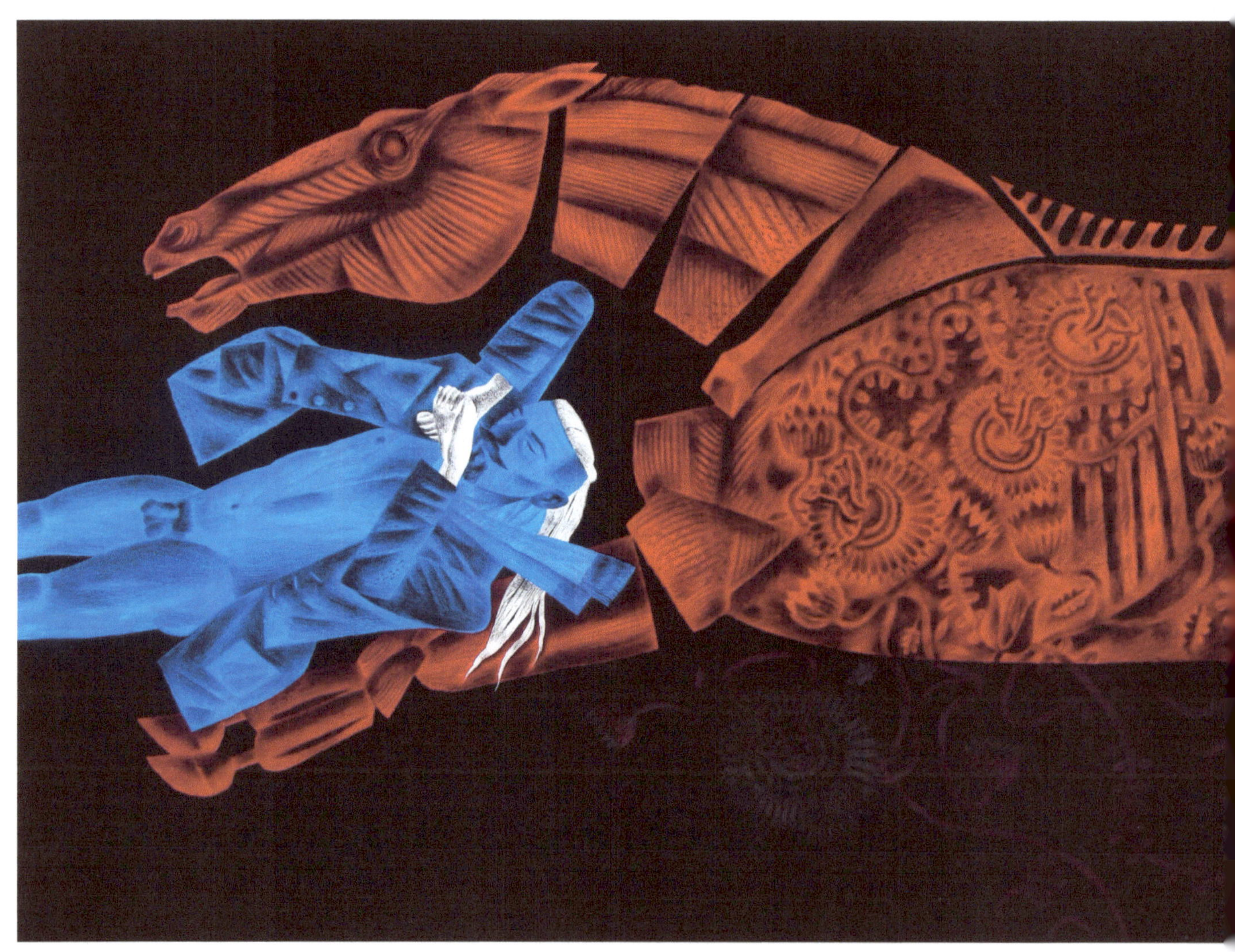

THE QUICKENING

We were alone on the hill
when my horse flew through me
Instead of stars my head trilling
with the Lord's passion
Pleasure in the dream

Tranquility of the Holy Thorn!
Tranquility of the Resurrected!

Scarlet as the moon over fields fallen
Scarlet as kisses sealed
My head fired with scars of lost youth
Innocence blooming into bruise
White comet! White prayer!

What lasts means slaughter and nakedness
The hill itself
Passion and its tendrils
in the beast's belly in the shadow of the dream

My daily urge walks a land without similarity teeming
That space called Distance and Here
Where red horses race faster than their shadows and...

Prayer Wheels of Passion!
Embroideries of Sleep!

Under the ragged mane
Under the boiling neigh
Under that which is and never becomes
Under that which always becomes and never is
Under the grey muzzle and the purple withers
I sought ripeness in the perishing

Pursuit bearing down
My hair a comet a scarf keeping the living alive
And the Here and the Distance quickening

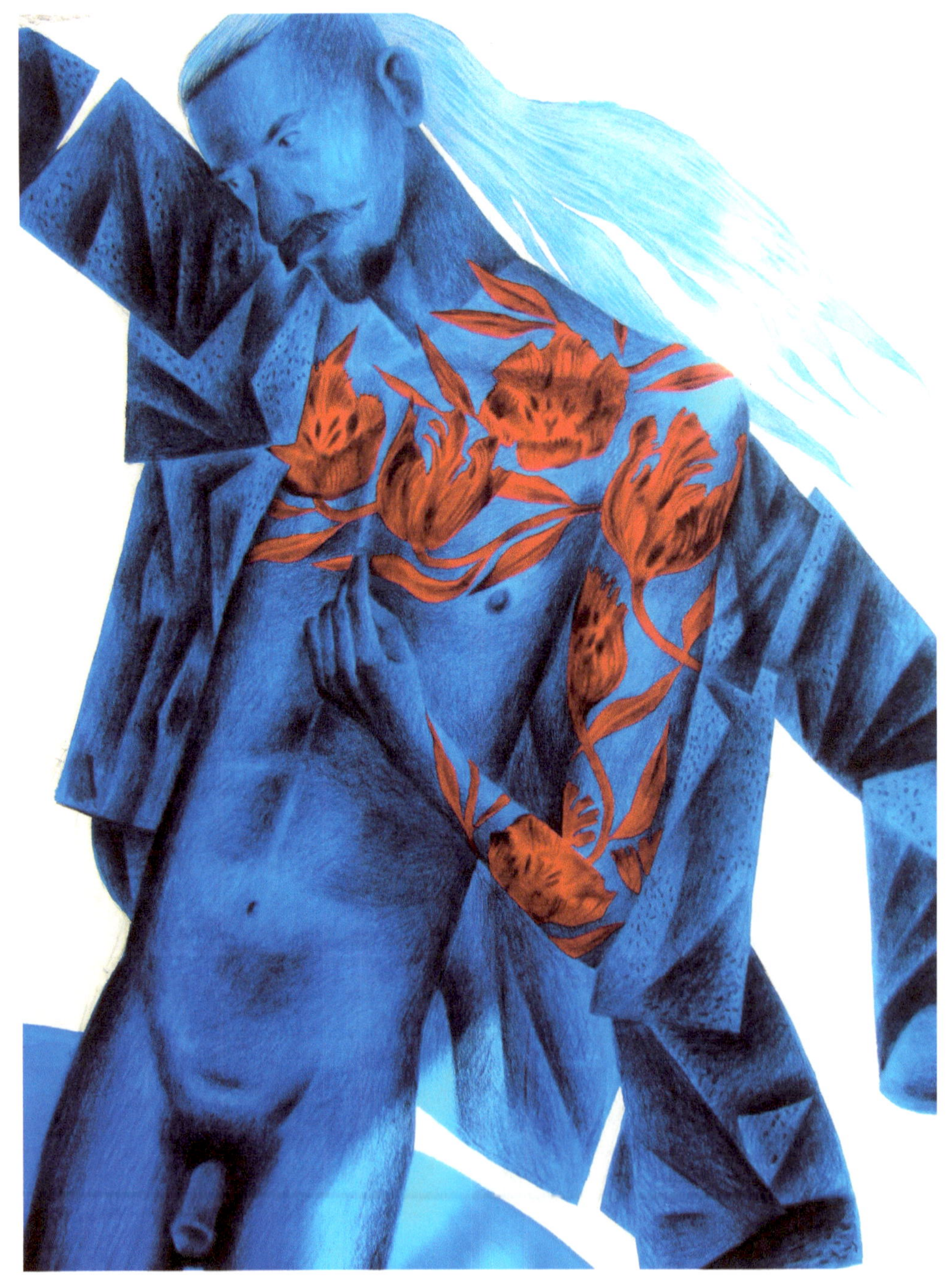

THE PROPHET ANSWERS THE MARE'S CALL: THE QUICKENING

My feet sprout wings
but all my eyes are shorn
My voice full
Syncopated by the dark

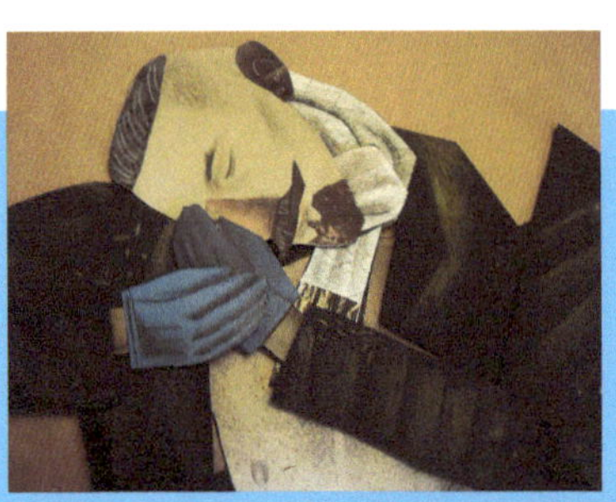

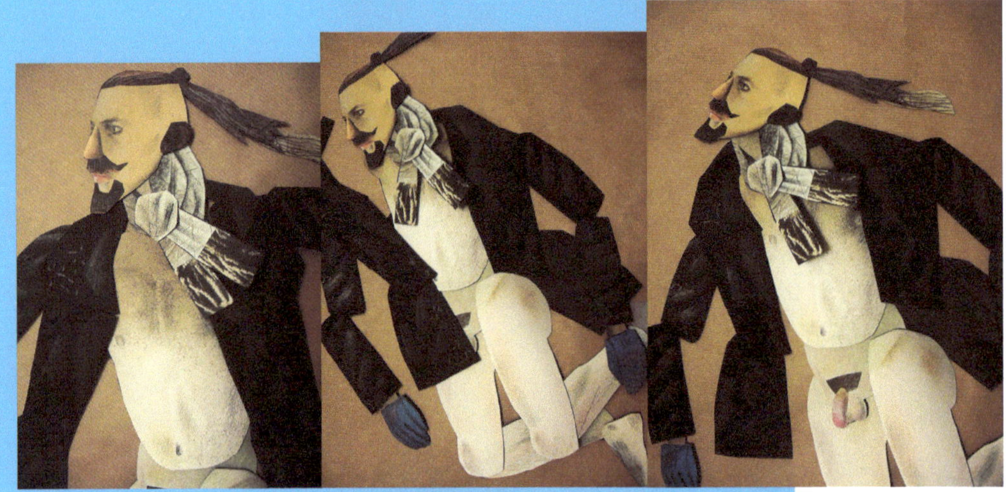

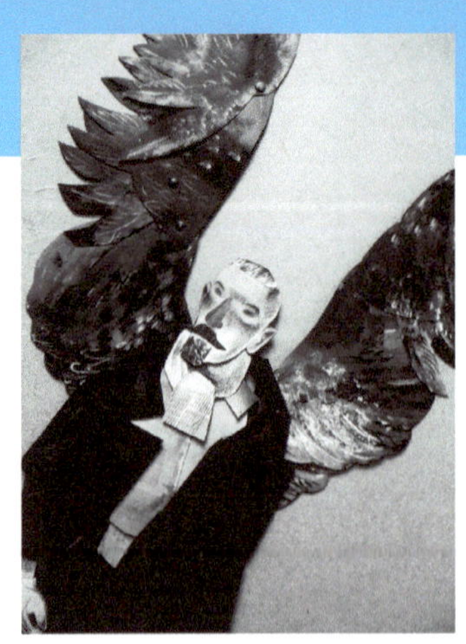

I TURN THE CORNER OF MY DREAM: JORDAN MORLEY MAQUETTE

I turn the corner of my dream and there you are
If you are paper then I am seeping quill
Tell me your deepest secret or the plainest fact
My scissory scissors zig-zagging your attack
The Lord-Maker stitching you in Time
Smoother than a saint's reliquary gold
Stringless susurrant sinew evoking and invoked

Tortuous midnight eyes
River a Jordan into my sweating
Beacon your revelatory fall then fall
into my arms pale prince Love's
Purest Grotesque Lust's Purest Angel
Contradictory Phoenix rise
Dance articulated dance
Join whole to whole
Kiss sinew bone fear
Kiss smoother than a saint's reliquary gold

The Lord-Maker stitching us in Time

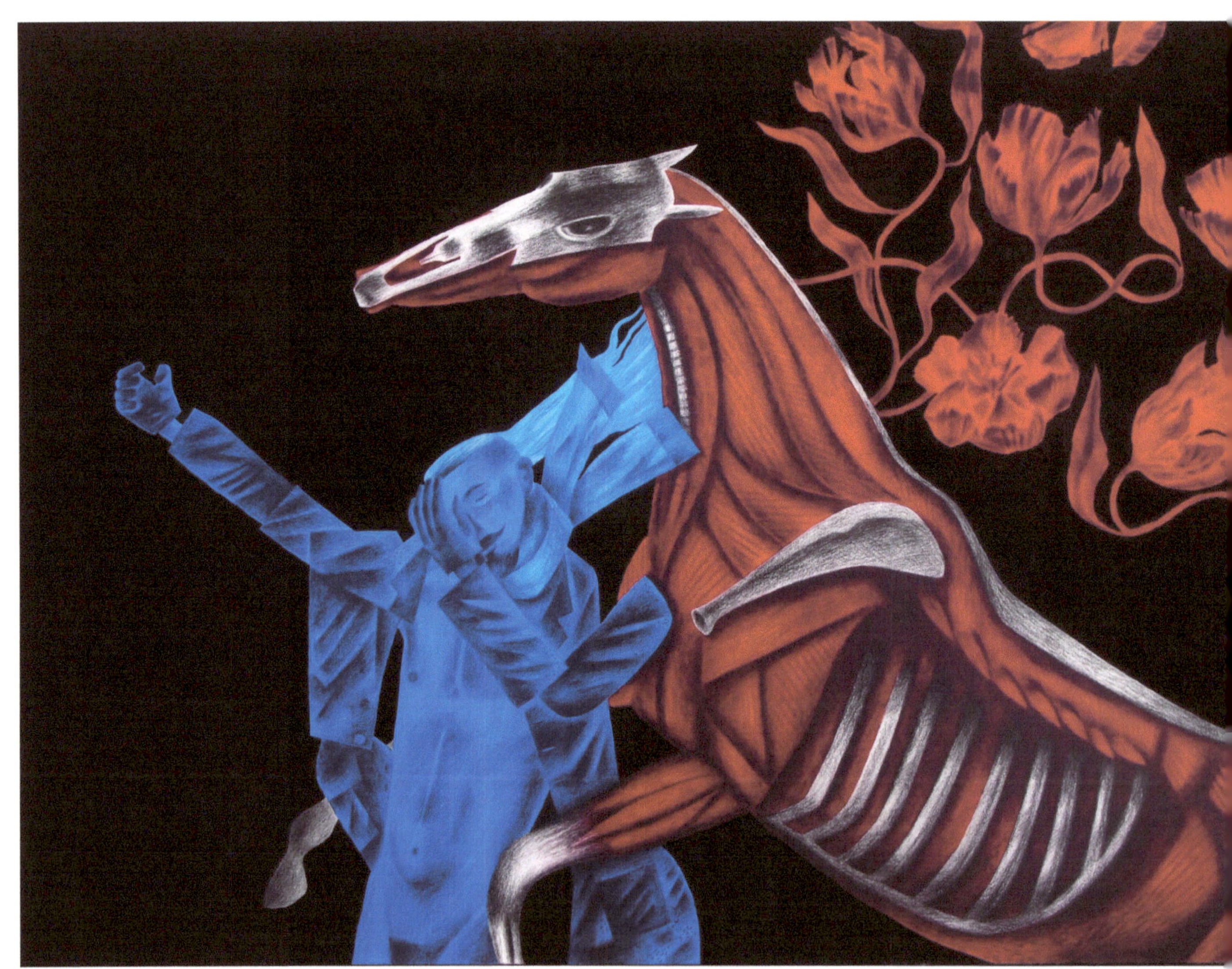

THE BIG BANG: RIVER JORDAN

The river's name in Hebrew is *Yarden*
Derived from *yarad* meaning "descend" or "flow down"

I am assembling and the wind is blowing

I wear no hat but warm my head with gleam

The prison of my clothes fast disappearing

Into the bat-wing motions wherein I fling

The vastness of my scarf teases my voice

Into a wilderness of wild and tender dances

I bend the wind I turn my forces

I lean and wonder through the Paradise I am

I am the first the primal constellating Adam

I am the pink at Solar System's center

I am comet burn listing toward the maelstrom

I whim my hands into a violet prayerful Jordan

I am a beastly bird with bones spontaneous

With stark disarming potential succor

I twist myself Gravities of Nothing

And from my Nothing the Universal forms

I am the Bastard Angel and the Virgin Devil

I am Again and Then and Was and Ever

I am assembling and the wind is blowing

I am the tale telling itself again

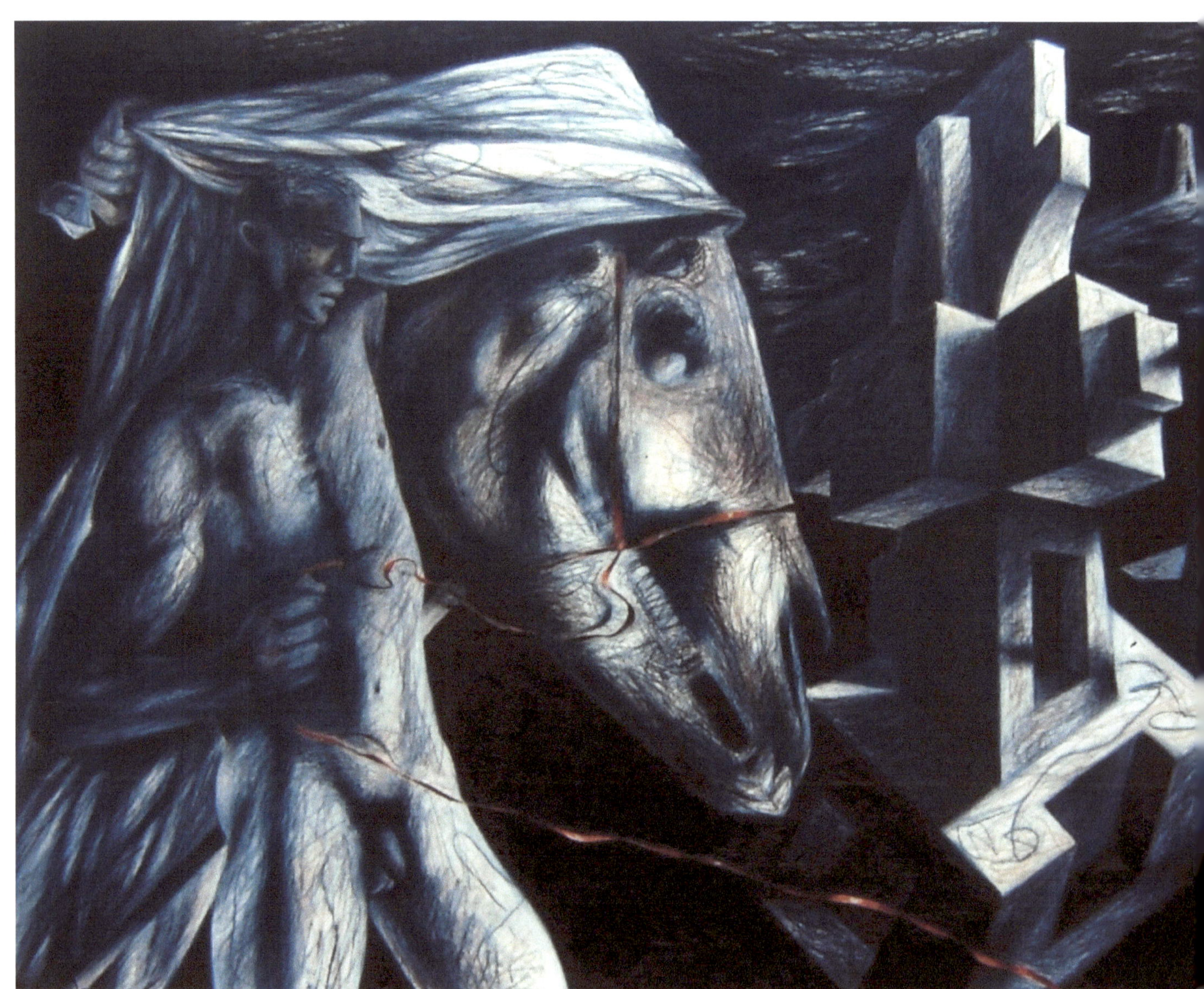

REGION OF SHROUDS

O Region of Shrouds
I see my death striding towards me
across rock my eyes cragging rock
slippery with fear and annunciations

If my heart shreds in some future dark
Trim me in gold
Brilliantine me in ruby and azure
Make me equine erect
Noble and pacing

I want to be inevitable like you a moon
the underworld's flaming towers
I want to be a shroud of shreds
thundering towards emptying

You even you love
the blue mountains
Zigzagging across hills and below Spring fields
Flowering blindingly joyously
without ever asking why

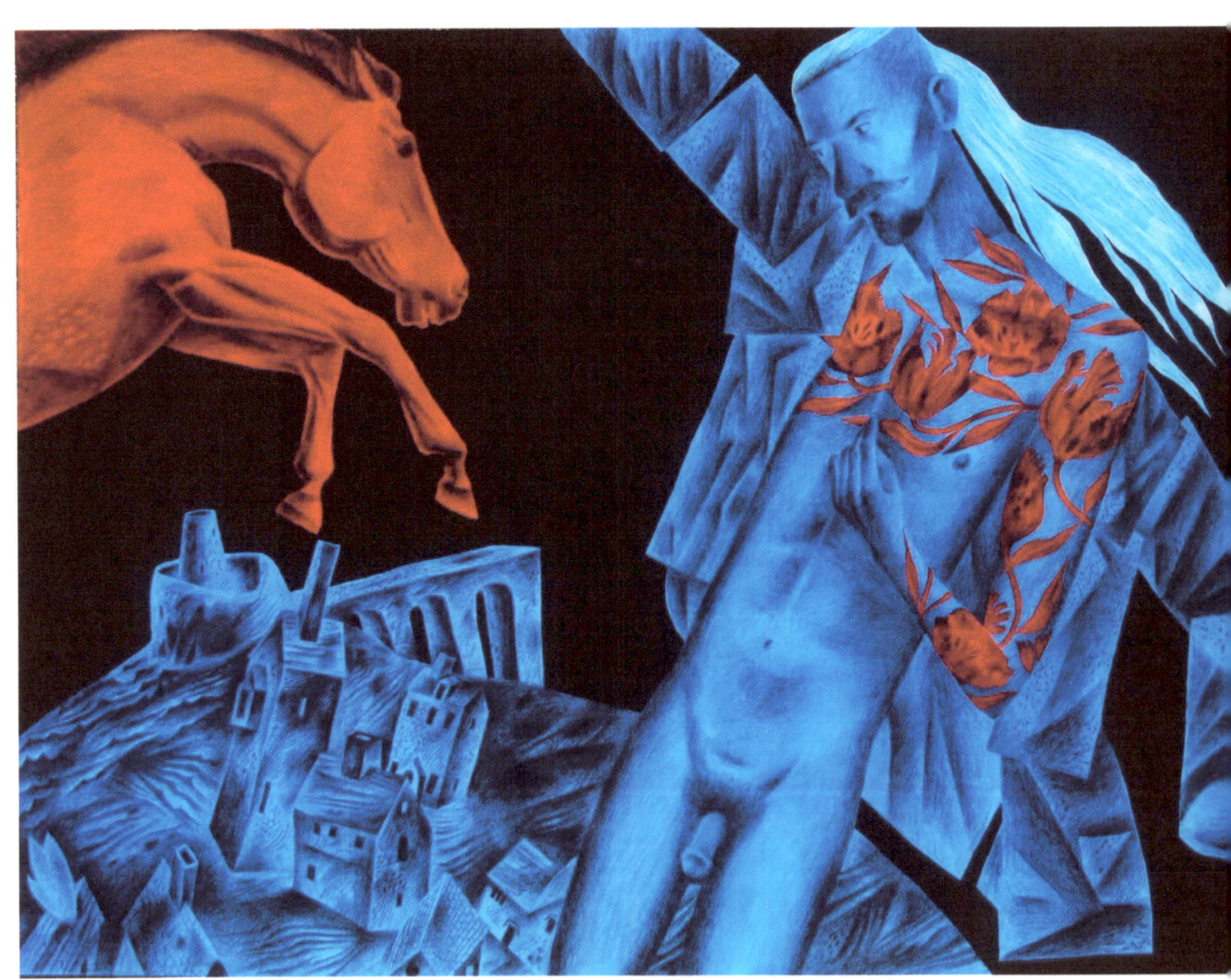

FLOWERING SKIN

Thou perceivest the Flowers put forth their precious Odours,
And none can tell how from so small a center comes such sweet,
Forgetting that within that Center Eternity expands
—William Blake

I have tended you under grey mare shanks
Under threadbare linen shrouds
Through whirlwind over abyss
Snarled in red-ribboned solstice rime
Stumbling falling shaving your likeness into memory

I have seen the wind in the stampede
Walked beside you in gloomy mournfulness
Hidden in candle-sputter and curtain-billow
Beneath coal-belching chimney and sinister-steep wobbling roofs
Chapel burning

This restless world
My hermitage of ruin of lapis
lazuli and mist

Father
I never knew what passion bloomed on your skin
but being a man and your Son
I know that bruise and bone born of the blood
that wretched wonderment stain
honey-milk sweet

I rise from the moonlight world
into twilight
fresh from the borderlands
with the river's blue arresting my thought

Skin's illusory boundary aim for providencial joy
Aim for the fiery ray in our eyes
Kiss these tattered frilly wounds
Breast and arm
Necklace and charm

And you
No skull on stick but majestic
Broken free
A wild beauty
My skin whispers to your springs of Living Water
Flowering earth outshining enemied darkness
And the wounds
the wounds
into April's May have ruby ridden

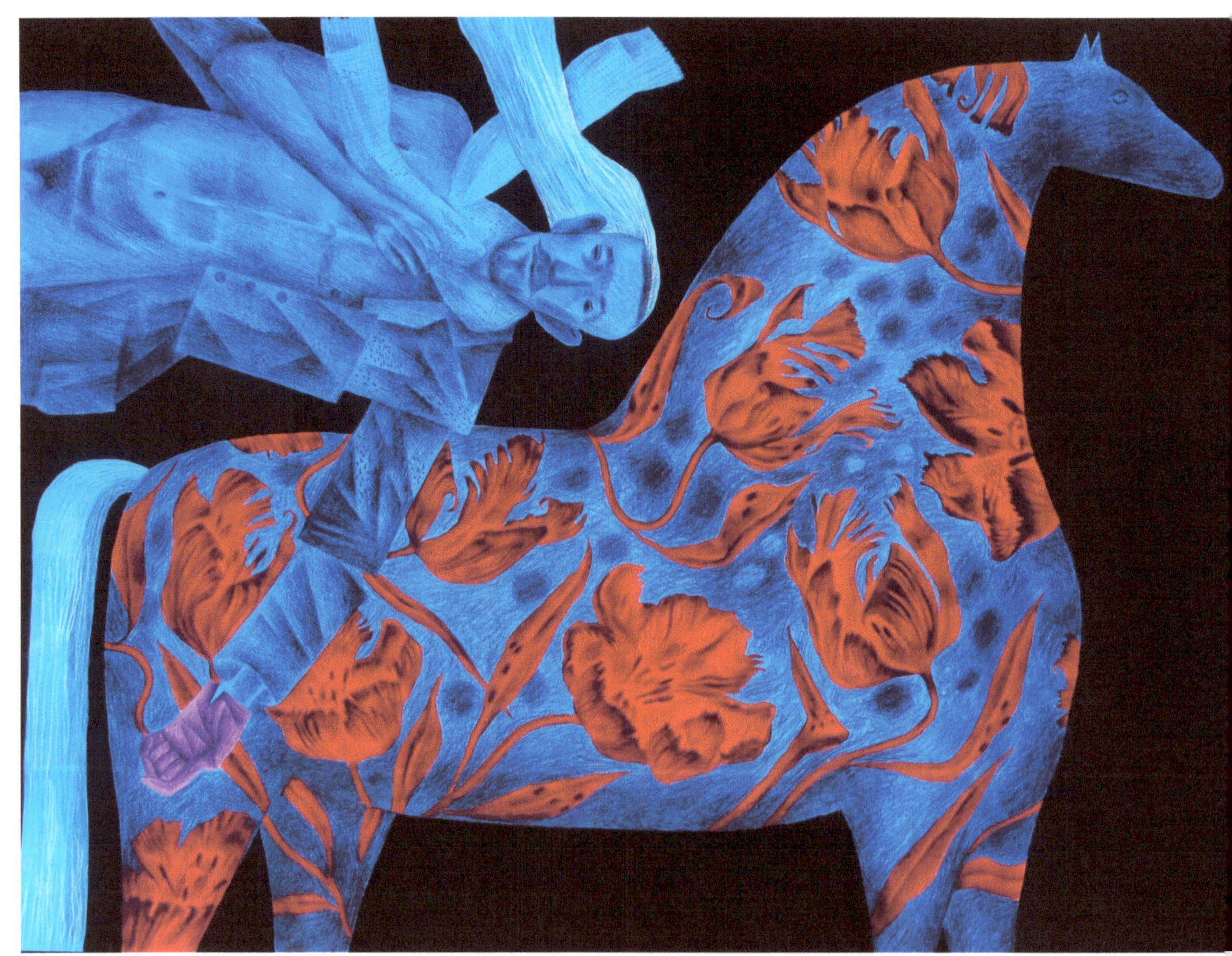

DRIFT

I cry silent revelation's first being
shaped by a primal hand upon the wall of a dank cave
flickering in light which half absolves half obscures me

Mari Mari Lywd having never spoken your name
your name becalms me
Right hand to heart left hand gloved closed holding a secret
Void's origin waiting to be opened
for you as you are for me my stalwart

A breeze from Heaven and you its muscular protector
catching my free-fall my gliding melancholia my drifting
stillness

Good for harsh things to become foliate
Good for blue blood's undercoat to absorb my bloody arabesques
Blood into flowers flowers into blood
River into your foliate serenity

I am tender as night in Heaven's black bowl
I am cubist roar made quiet
I am Lord-Maker and Beating Heart to your Waiting

Who shall command who follow
We together under the Canopic plain
We whispering each other in our wild warriors' canters
In our fragrant gentilities

I am thinking whether I love you do you love me
This love that goes back to the first humans
ancient as the sea's sweet syllables whispering the yew

I am thinking I love you you love me
Seeing nothing I see all
Feeling the Void I feel the Fullness
I drift unlost to you
Mari Mari Lwyd
Radiance assembled

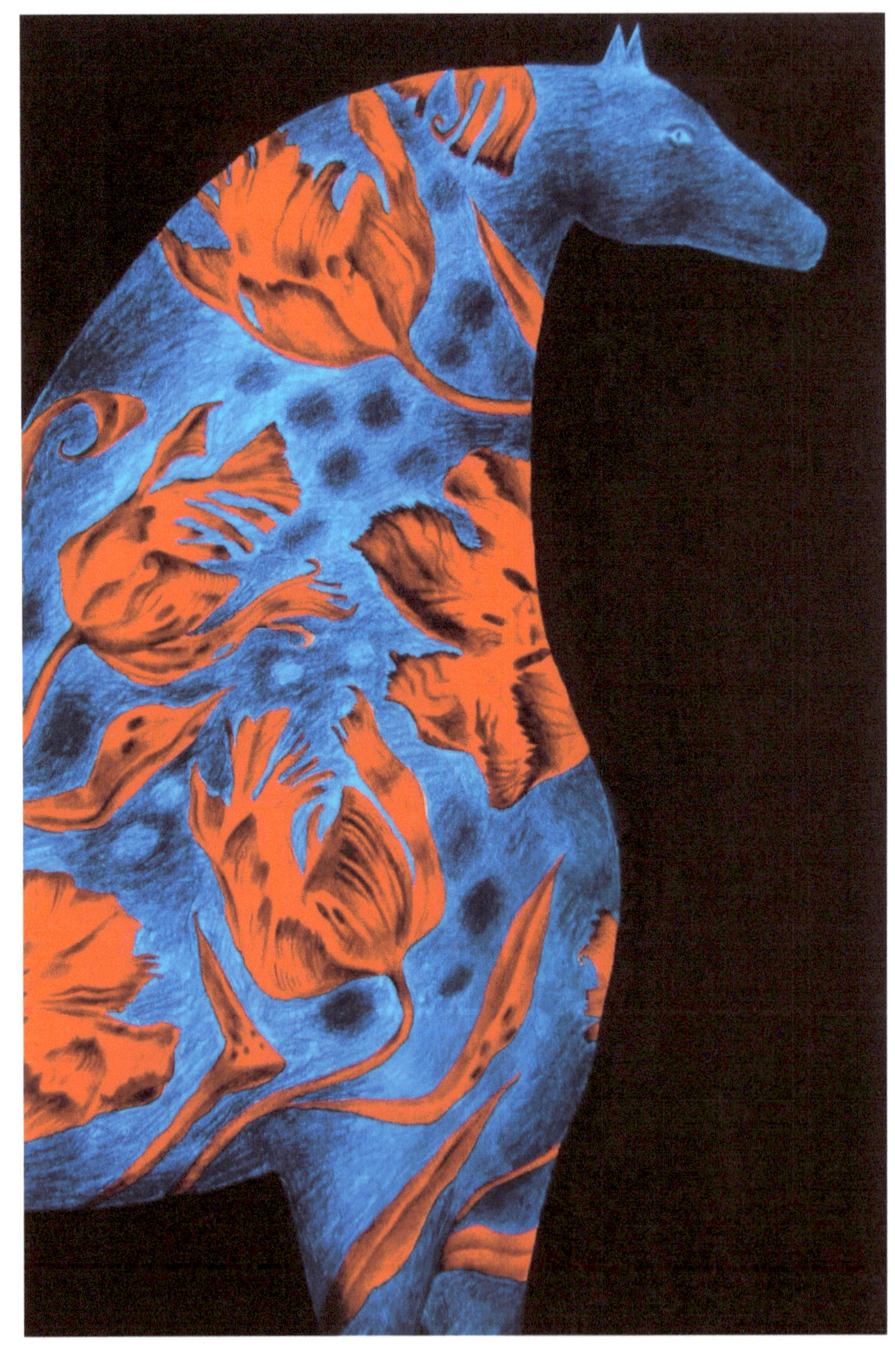

THE GRIM REAPER APPEARS AS A NIGHT-FLOWER

Delicate thief!
I thought your roar something
children imagined in a storm
Instead you light up the night meteoric
I hear you flash
Then all quiet
Done

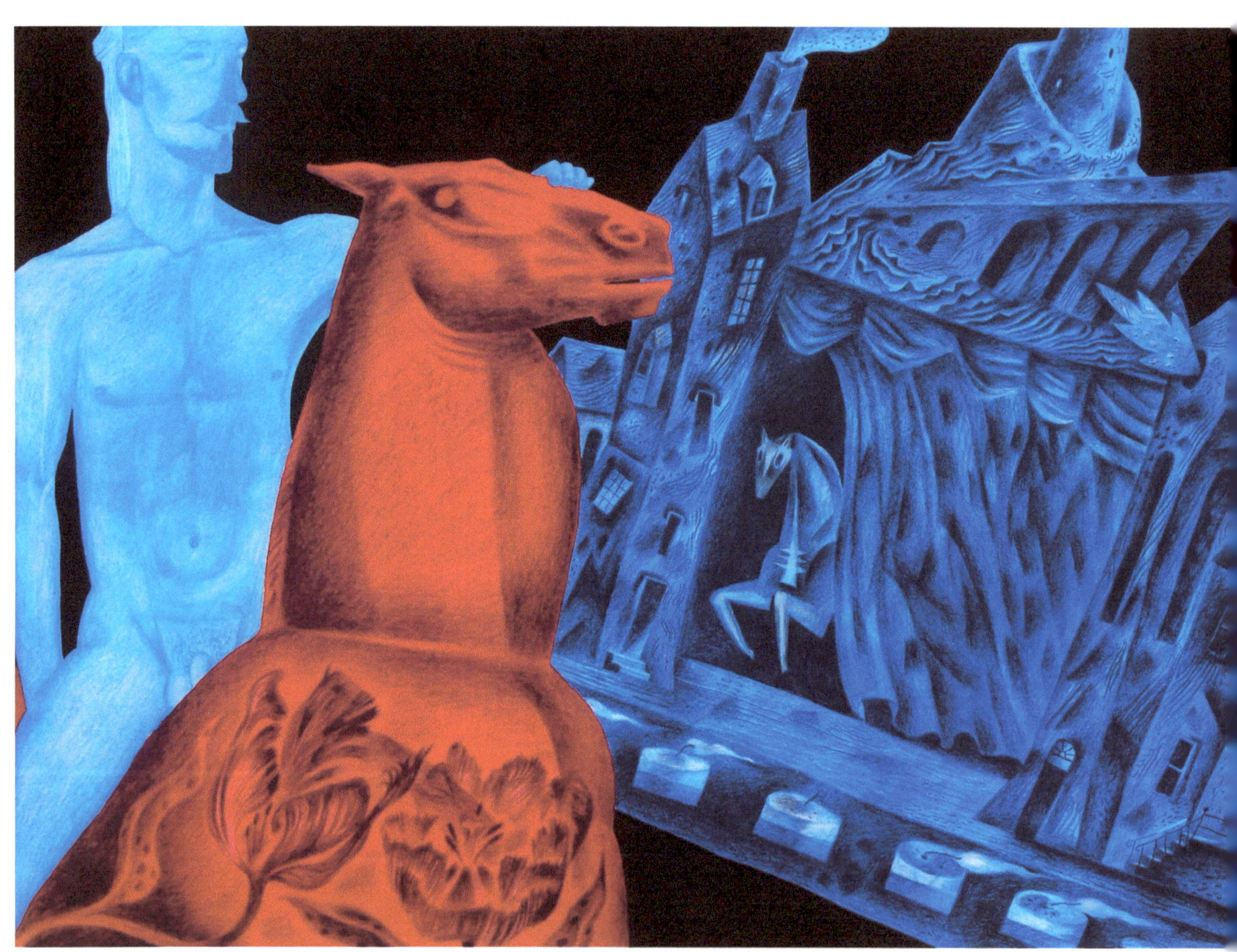

VEIL

The houses fall behind us to their knees,
the streets bend slantingly to meet us,
the squares give way: we take hold of them,
with our horses rushing like a rain.
                    —Rainer Maria Rilke

And when the mare I'd mounted
we roamed long lonely barrens
searching for village and tower
seeking the memory of my father's passing
Bone house rearing into inferno
Manes of Ardor Manes of Memory

And when the village came into view
I bore naked the signs inherited
bluing those fears away
into a radiant run
once charred and skinned
now whispering me into blossom-bracing blue
sulfurous purple-vined with new life
Vines of Green
Veins though perilous alive

I fear peril nevermore
I see the old toy mare on a children's stage
And I riding forth
leanness and handsomeness my sword

Lwyd you searched and knew me
knew my downsitting and my uprising
You gave me the road and lay me down
All my ways are yours to know
Veil sundered
Veil blown open in cyclone
Wind from Death's dark
Wind from Under

The Under my friend
My horse my lover my guide
Steady as a raven in a tree
Steady as my father's noble death
Steed steady on
Come Through Come Through

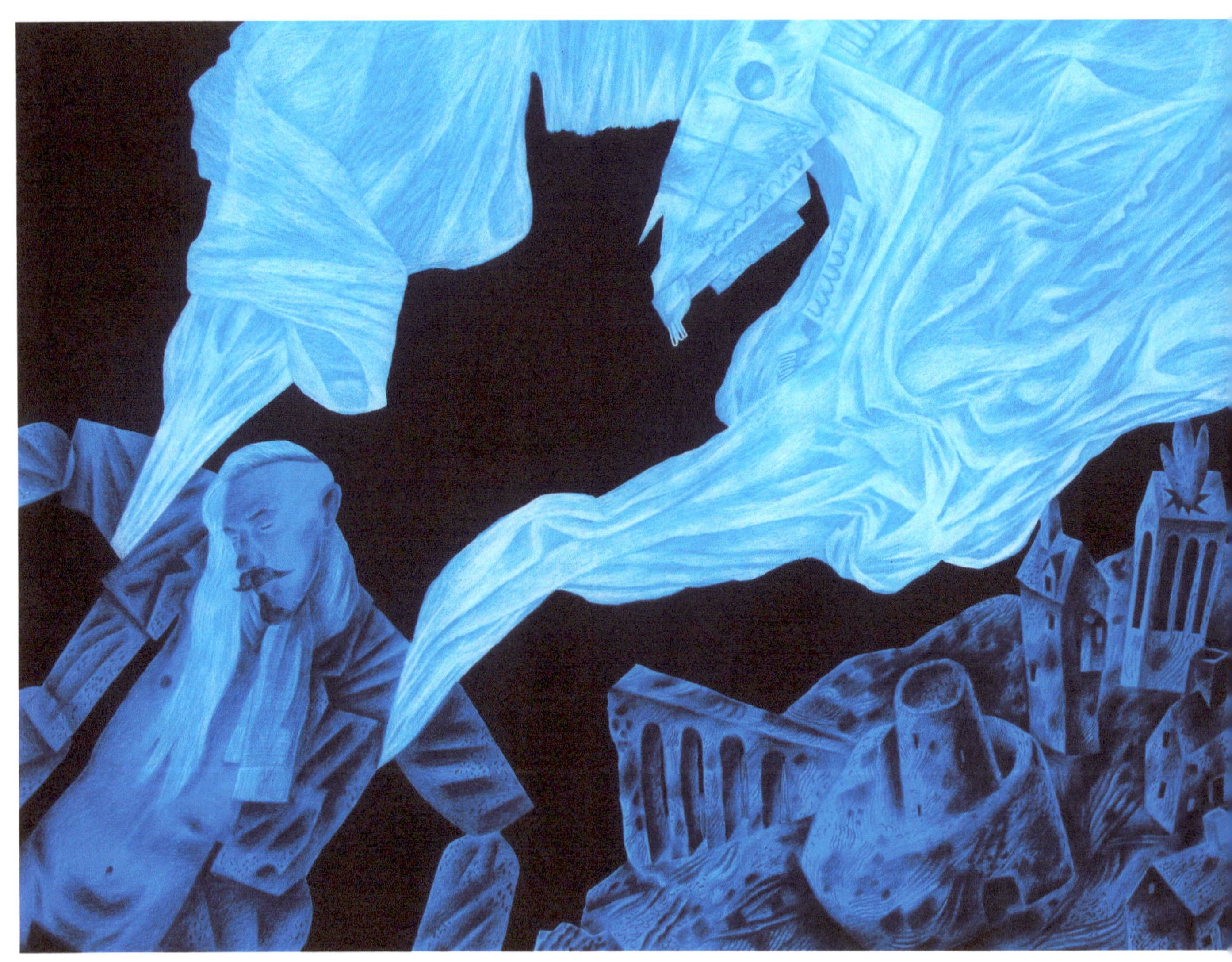

PEGASUS

Let me dress you for a funeral
Let me decorate your grave with tulips and owl leavings
Let me swift as wind fast as water-wave bathe you in wonder
Let me in eyelid flick gust quantum breath over you
Let me descend sleep into you
Let me clatter my bones in mesmeric song
Let me cool you with my wings' cold fire

I am Pegasus Spectral
Pegasus Reversed
I am your nightmare-longing toward dust
Be not afraid

Terrible the ways of men
Terrible the rib-cage's prison Noon's paralyzing auguries

My seed crescents the widest delta
My grave the blackest richest loam
And tulips await you on my stony ground

Your dance blesses you
Your devotion blesses you
My mystery blesses you
You my foal seasoned for sacrifice
Ripe for reckonings and reversals bindings and elopements

Hypnotics of your white eyelashes
Purification of your head's whitest hairs

Stop shaking
Every funeral prophesies resurrection
In quiet you will hear cymbals bang and clang
Stampedes crushing mind-forg'd manacles

I will instruct you while dressing you
I will suit you for a crown

Here hides the secret your uttermost desire
Moist as the grave moist as the birth canal
Moist as your weeping your dancing

When I release you ravens populate the mountains
The almond prospers the cloister again

Liberty and Love the two Great Secrets
Making the Divine Mind smile
Making Death forget himself and sing
Paradise regained
Without contraries is no progression

Your hair standing on end
The Namer and the Named

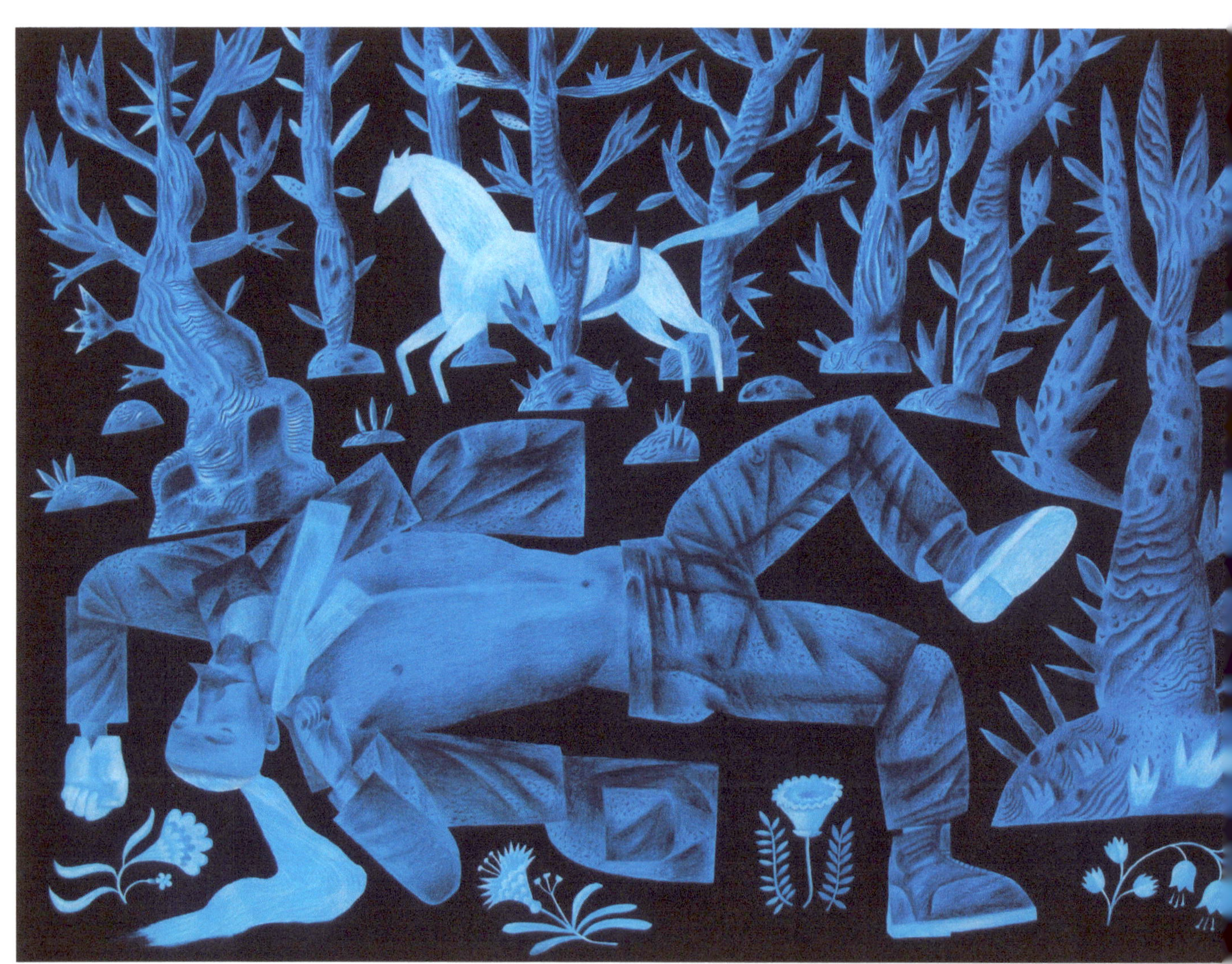

PALE HORSE

Fair Jordan lay on cold cold ground
His vision there to see
His steed stood guard within the wood
Blind Jordan in reverie

A sphere of light rose in his eye
Within a raven flaming
A voice rang down the tower tall
To consecrate his naming

Rise up rise up sweet Jordan fair
Your journey's near its ending
Your sickened plight transforms tonight
Your heart no more rending

Fair flowers sprout from Mari's tread
Each one a fear forgotten
Now you are one with fear and dread
You'll be no more ill gotten

Pale man Pale horse beloveds rise
Division's an earthly dreaming
For you have found in wood and flower
The Truth behind all seeming

More This than That more Now than Then
More Yes than No   No Never
Relinquish grief Revive and dance
Your trance welcomes new being

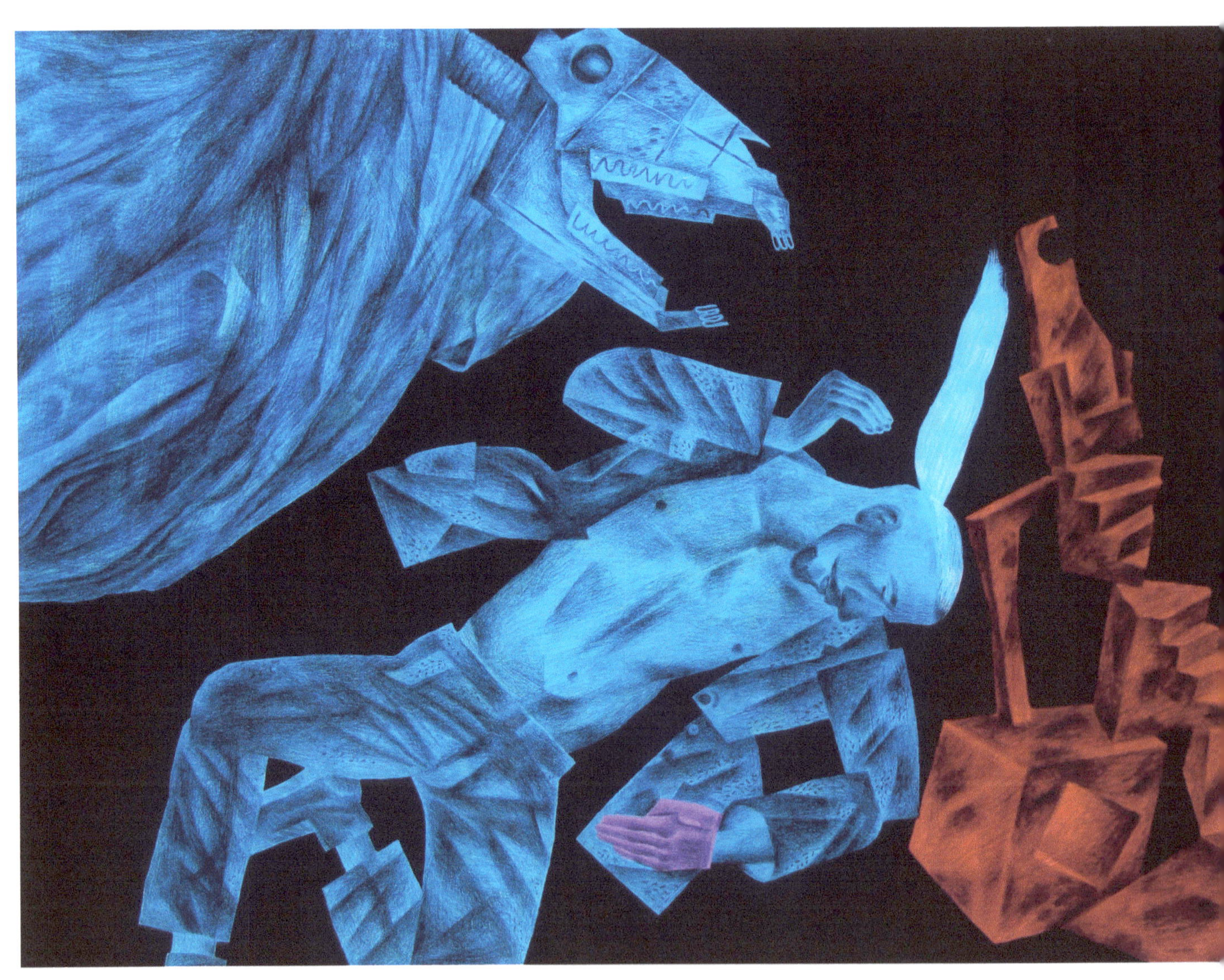

THE CITADEL

Thus I come to the Citadel
not knowing what fate awaits me
Throwing myself from the parapet my previous life
The brief before

Sleep gnaws at my belly
Hunger at my soul
My hands dance mandibles of the fiend
Mudras of the saints

I know I know
when I awaken the fortress will become a beacon
Everything's eternal afterward

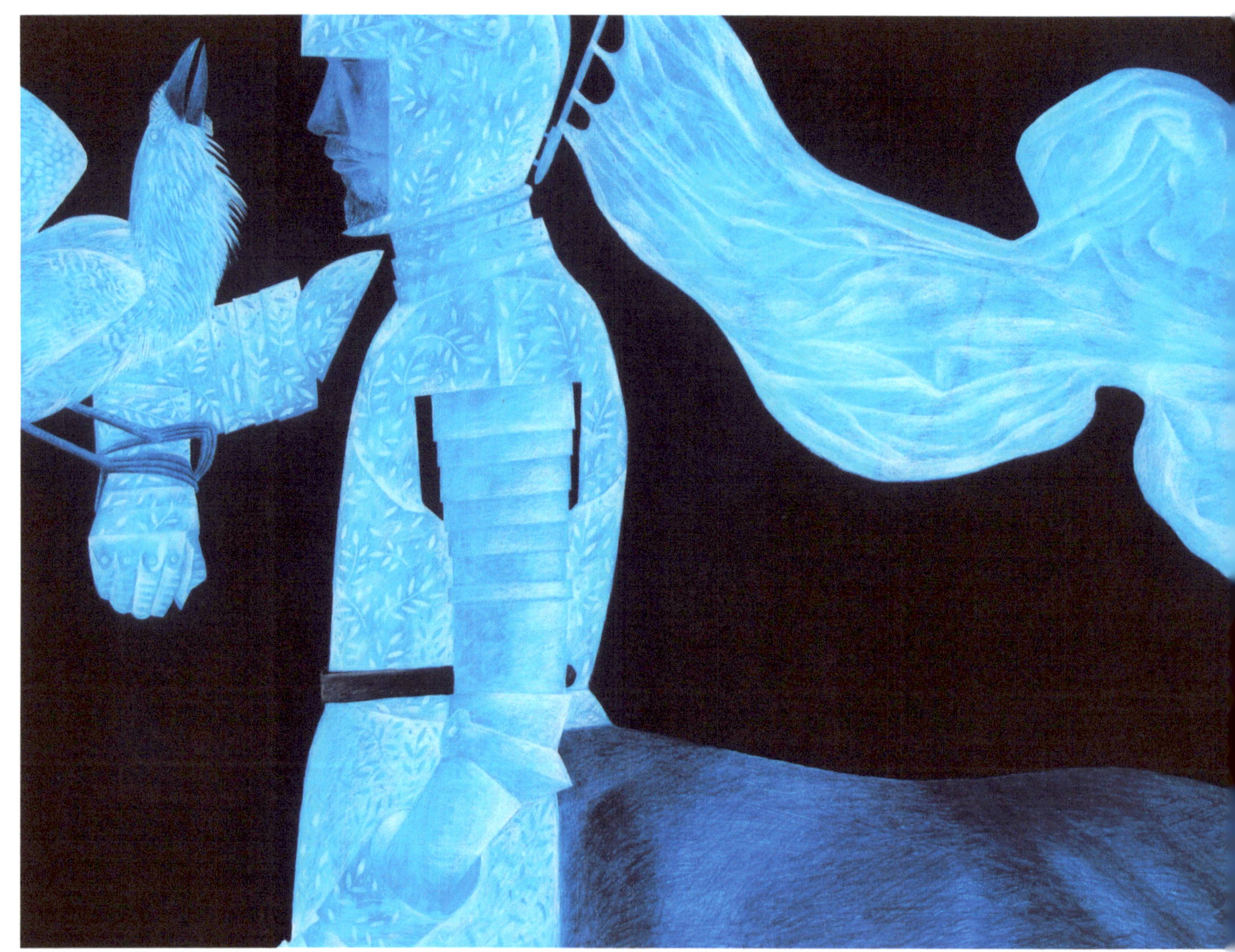

MEETING THE CENTAUR: HORSEMAN

I skirt the black and put my flowers on
I trail a path from tower to tomb
I skirt the tomb and enter married bower
I hold the horse's rein and ring the runes

Fair muscled centaur redder than the stain
Dancer and dance mummer to my whim
Embrace me churn me in a cosmic shower
I am the Dark One all more beautiful

Why does the world exist nothing to nothing comes
Assuming form I do myself undone
My blaze of tulips parrot galaxies and none
My foliate armor my wedding pendant flown
My gloves of hammered sprigs of vegetative force

My eyes gazing from original springs
I germinate and shepherd within the Green
And Blue my talisman to my dying self
And horse myself into reviving God

Blue Prince ethereal
Authority dignified
I am the Dark One all more beautiful

Are you terrestrial or real or both
Saintly pearl ringing in the rune

I know you sister mother daughter
I know you brother father son

Here is my beard it grows like water down
Here hangs my tender scepter sleeping with its crown
Here my snowy helmet my glittery earth
Are you my witness or my husband now

My raven whitened by transfigured blood
My soul sense heightened by prey I've sought and found
In Jordan's currents delight and stillness reign
Fair muscled centaur in white we are as one

Why does the world exist something to something comes
Assuming form I do myself become
Are you there prancing Grecian young
Remember the Secret Commonwealth we share

I skirt the black and put my flowers on
I trail a path from tower to tomb
I skirt the tomb and enter married bower
I hold the horse's rein and ring the runes

I am the Dark One all more beautiful
I germinate and shepherd within the Green
And Blue my talisman to my dying self
And horse myself into reviving God

Here ends the last exile of the common man

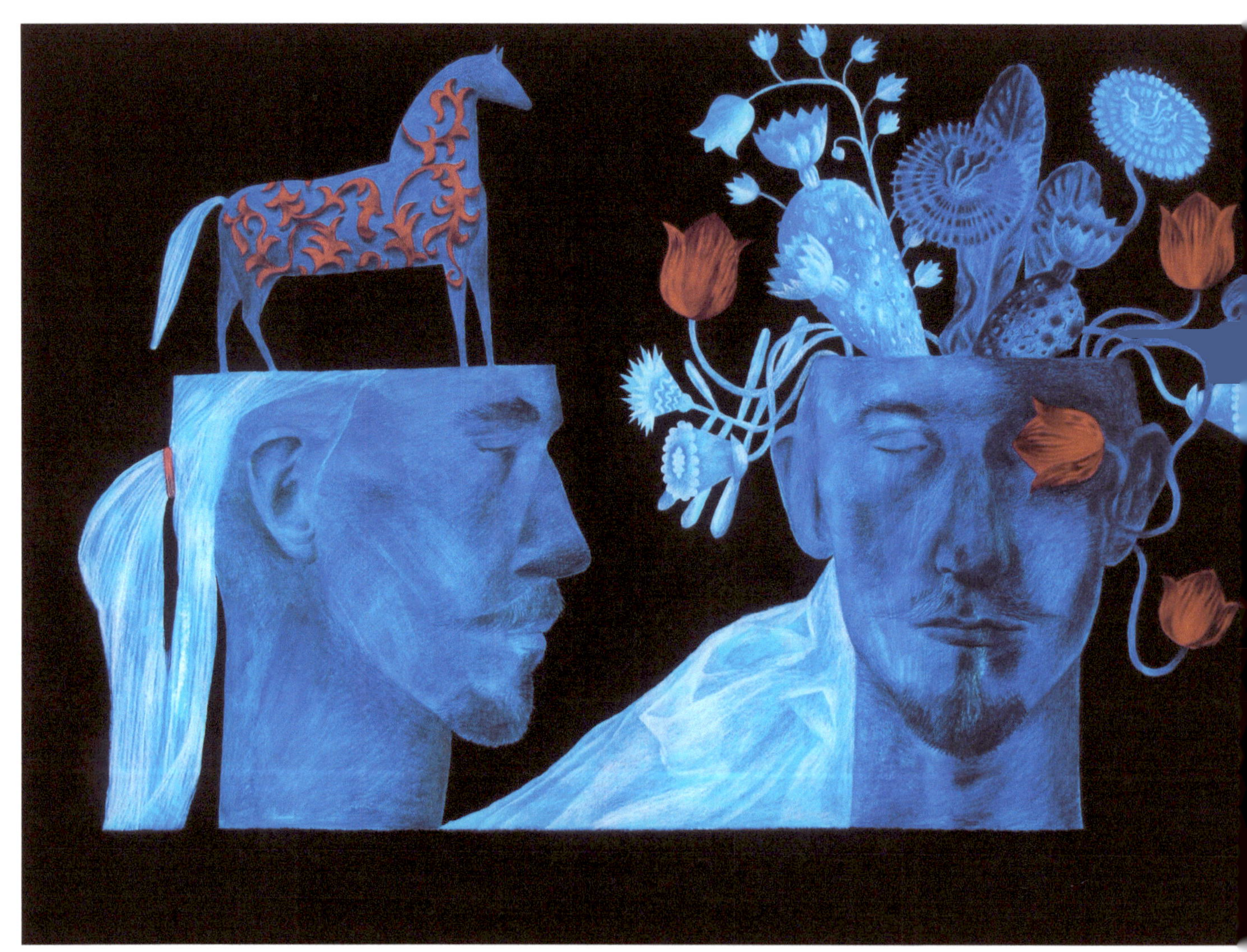

BIRTH

The beautiful man is dreaming
All shrouds transfigured all childish dreads dissolved
I am the man the horse the horse the man
I am the dream dreaming itself the race done
All man all human all Nature but Beyond

Along the rippling midnight stallion thrum
I am the Dark One's dancing veil
I am Love's shrouded truthful face

The super natural man

I have no secrets left to tell
you glean them all
You hear them in the salmon's run
The badger peering from her ground the dog at play
The child in mother's arms
The stallion's stance
Eden's verdant tendril surge my polished glance

You who have not known me know me now
I am fecundity in blue
I am Love's shrouded truthful face
The azure's fiery gallant youthful locks

Too many words for I am just a face
Altered by every canter every prance

Altered by Holy Sleep and Hand-in-Glove
I am fecundity in blue
I offer all and nothing imparting Grace

Mystery of Heaven Secrets of the Sea
Riddle of the Land have all revealed become
I am the bluest eye and angel wing
The call to Holy Marriage and to prayer
The holy navel and the holy well
I am the veil's immortal fields
Death Dream and Birth envelop me
I am the Dark One's circling veil

How many tumbles makes a saint
How many coarse meals fractured ankles how many stones
How many crashing oaks how many tears
after their bloom has gone fragrance the room

Eyes universes in the geometric dark the dreamer's head
Pale boy whose quicksilver hair becomes the shroud
The poem of Seraphic Time and Timelessness revealed
Cold comet harmony radiance of unceasing Earth
I am the unsubstantial heart grown into Now

The super natural man

Too many words for I am just a face
A mask of fret and innocence made world
World teeming with ten thousand galloping things
that shoot and flower always ever were

Touch soft these lips these eyes they speak a human tongue
Listen hushed in ultramarine as tender crows
weep midnight sighs within the Sacred Grove
The beautiful man is dreaming

Embroideries of Sleep!
Tranquility of the Holy Thorn!
Tranquility of the Resurrected!

All shrouds transfigured all childish dreads dissolved
I am the Dark One's dancing veil
I am Love's shrouded truthful face

I am the Bastard Angel and the Virgin Devil
I am Again and Then and Was and Ever
I am assembling and the wind is blowing
I am the unsubstantial heart grown into Now

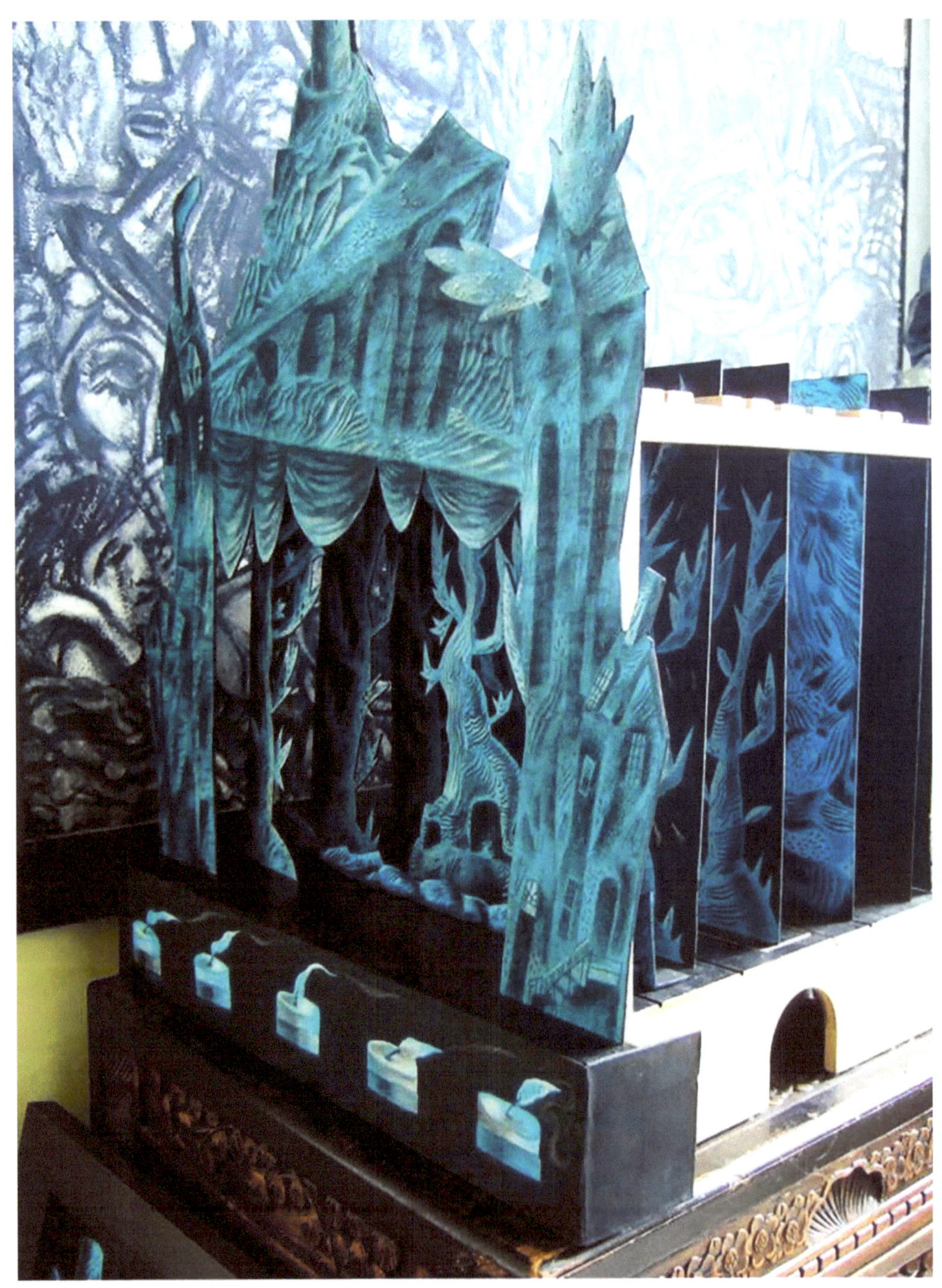

DARK MOVEMENTS

                              —J. N. Chubb

Out of dark movements always comes the beast
Be it dragon, raven, horse, bull, unicorn, or sacred sow
From the theater of wants needs and fairy dusts
Steps the starborn dressed in animal presence
Wings made numinous by nocturnal thoughts

Hidden in herald's guise a man more uncanny than light
More canny than beauty can bear and just as tall
Leads stallion white and sapphire mare to trough
Where waters yonder glister blue-black the sacred trust

From stifling thorny grove toward clashing fire
From woodland perilous the walking trees
To village torn asunder in their wake
The maddening spark the nightmare's cawing gyre

The starborn's heart to genesis aroused
For deathless death the end of time and sleep
He welcomes from his newborn innocence
The something far the something near
The something that he always knew to be

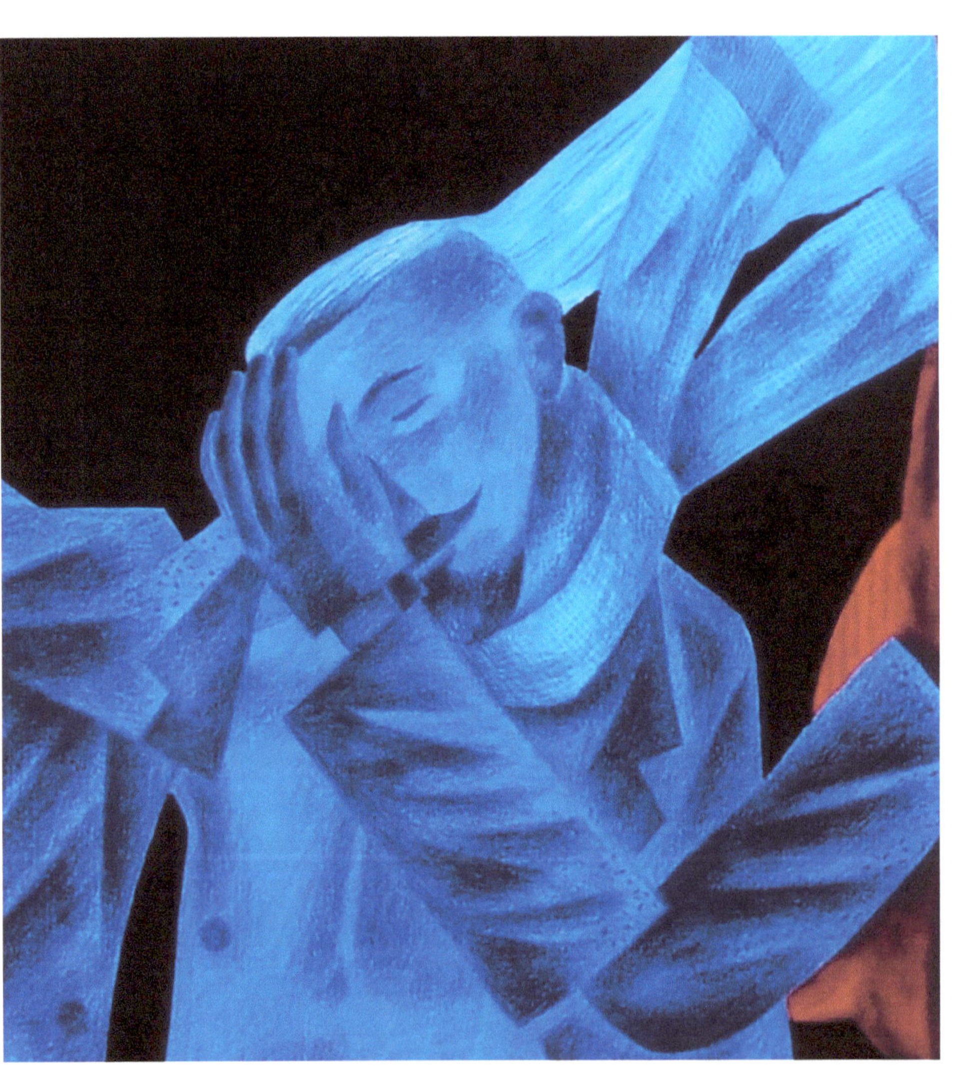

I DREAMED A DREAM:
THE POETRY OF *SPECTRAL PEGASUS / DARK MOVEMENTS*

As I walk'd through the wilderness of this world, I lighted on a certain place where was a Den, and I laid me down in that place to sleep; and as I slept, I dreamed a Dream.
—John Bunyan, *Pilgrim's Progress*

In our heads surely all of us are simultaneously many things: child and adult hand in hand, the innocent and experienced journeying together. It's just that too many forget that, or don't understand it or express it. But the artists, the poets and the makers…we must express it, if we are to do our jobs.
—Clive Hicks-Jenkins

Walk with me beside me arm-in-arm / Let's watch the twilight tower lurch into sapphire
—Jeffery Beam, *Spectral Pegasus*

✾✾✾✾✾✾✾✾

Although the Welsh artist Clive Hicks-Jenkins and the American poet Jeffery Beam didn't meet until May 2017, more than two years after they began and completed their collaboration, they are undoubtedly part of the same mystical lineage, which values, above all things, nature and the power of the imagination. Myth, magic, and mystery transform the ordinary into the extraordinary in each man's work—the world, in all its strangeness and beauty, revealed.

The advent of a major new exhibition, *Dark Movements*, in 2015, saw Hicks-Jenkins confronting for a second time the most significant theme of his career, one inspired by his father's childhood terror of the Mari Lwyd of Welsh mumming tradition—a survival of the Celtic and Roman veneration of horses that once could be found in similar celebrations throughout Britain and mainland Europe. The cult of the Mari centres round a mare's skull bedecked in sheet and ribbons, which is carried from door to door to mark the passing of the longest nights of midwinter. The Mari is accompanied by a band of mummers, in the guise of the dead, who, in a rhyming contest with the people indoors, seek admission into the houses of the living. Upon gaining entry, food and drink are enjoyed by all and blessings bestowed for the coming year.

Clive Hicks-Jenkins writes of his father's childhood experience of the Mari Lwyd tradition, "When my father was a child, his community was still a rural one, where winter nights were lit only by oil lamps and the coming of the Mari would have been keenly anticipated by families with few entertainments to distract them after the labour of long, hard days... My father recalled the spark and clatter of hob-nailed boots on the cobbled path, the keening squeeze-box and the beat of drum underlying the clamour of the Mari's bells as the beast careered toward the house, led by a man in tail-coat and cock-feathered top-hat... He described the glint of the sawn-off bottoms of beer bottles rammed into the skull's eye-sockets, and the hinged and clacking jaws, out of which a beribboned ladle appeared to take offerings of coins. Most of all, he described his horror when the throng was invited into the parlour; the press and the reek and the noise. The Mari bucked and span in circles, then chased his grown-up sisters about the house, accompanied by shrieks of excitement and the crash of overturned tables and breaking china. This was not a polite occasion. Rules were broken and anarchy prevailed. No wonder little Trevor was appalled! And he never forgot, his recollection vivid in old age not because of repeated tellings...for he had never spoken of it...but because it had frightened the wits out of him, and the memory had stayed fresh."

Stories are how we make sense of the world. The Mari Lwyd, in Hicks-Jenkins' original telling of the tale, created between 1998-2001 and exhibited in 2001, became both a highly personal meditation on the death of his father and an elegy to the friends and colleagues he had lost during his theatre career to the AIDS epidemic. Catriona Urquhart, a longtime friend of the artist and his father, wrote the poetic text that accompanied the original body of work, which became known as *The Mare's Tale.* The Old Stile Press published the poems in 2001; Catriona's words made all the more poignant when we learn of her early death, only a few years later.

When an artist is setting off anew on a journey to the borderlands, where the Mari roams, a poet companion is necessary to answer the Night Mare's challenges with his rhymes. Beam heard the clarion call through the dark night, where he was dwelling, and greeted the Spectral Pegasus like a friend. He confesses: "I feared I was written out and had taken sanctuary in my studies. The Mari Lwyd became a beacon in the darkness for me; one which ignited an explosion of creativity."

The Appalachian Scots-Irish and Cherokee blood, which flows through Beam's veins, shaped him into a rough-hewn Seer, drawn to the songs and stories of older worlds. His earliest influences were the "resident Celtic goddesses…my paternal grandmother and my mother with her second-sight", whose abiding legacy "allows me visions and to believe in them, no matter how the practical Calvinist and Pennsylvanian-Dutch sides of my heritage…might fight against it."

From the child is born the lyric and mythic poet of whom the critic Chad Driscoll writes: "The natural world retains its otherness in Jeffery's imagination, monsters still run wild through the wilderness, and God may still be sought there."

The liminal landscape of the Mari Lwyd, as imagined by Hicks-Jenkins, is a place where Beam, like many gay men of his generation, has walked: "The invitation to join this pilgrimage offered me a space to elaborate and sing my own unfolding—just as Clive was doing. It felt good to have a companion with me on the road this time, one who is a soul brother to me. I sensed where he needed to travel, as it was a journey I wanted to take as well." Poets and painters have long been magnetised by travelling to the edges of things.

The poems and paintings of *Spectral Pegasus / Dark Movements* emerged in an alchemical process, which took everybody involved by surprise. Separated by an ocean, Hicks-Jenkins, Beam, and their model/muse, the dancer Jordan Morley, invented new modes of collaboration. Poems and images of sketches and partially finished paintings flew back and forward, each new expression influencing the next stages of work. In New York, Morley steeped himself in all *The Mare's Tale* lore that had gone before and presented photographs of his improvised performances within the newly developing scenarios. In Wales, Hicks-Jenkins built maquettes of his muse and arranged them into compositions in preparation for making studies and paintings. An engaged audience watched and contributed to the creative process through social media.

In North Carolina, Beam, freed from a long silence, started to write, "The voices coming and going and elaborating and questioning were palpable. I heard Catriona and Clive's father calling and responding to me, but I also sensed the neigh, the moving of the Mari Lwyd and the excitement of her gender, color, and form changes acting as a voice in the journey. I felt alive again. Totally scared and disbelieving in the poems that were emerging, I gave myself over to a sort of automatic writing."

To readers of Beam's work, *Spectral Pegasus / Dark Movements* may come as a surprise if they are not familiar with his earliest poems. These new poems hark back to early works such as the poems in his first book *The Golden Legend* and the Surrealist prose poem sequence *Submergences* (and an unpublished student manuscript *The Wizard's Foot*). In *Spectral Pegasus* he has shed his often elegant, sometimes aphoristic, Objectivist, concisely crisp, Gnostic and Zen-like poems for the burning sensations of words and images piled onto, flooding over, and colliding with each other, but with a difference. It is as if Hicks-Jenkins' paintings knocked a long-stored magical elixir off Beam's poetic shelf and into his inkpot. The Sorcerer's Apprentice, indeed!

Religious historian Mircea Eliade linked shamanism to the creation of lyric poetry in his book *Shamanism: Archaic Techniques of Ecstasy*: "It is…probable that the pre-ecstatic euphoria [of the shaman] constituted one of the universal sources of lyric poetry… The purest poetic act seems to re-create language from an inner experience that, like the ecstasy or the religious inspiration of 'primitives,' reveals the essence of things."

Beam acknowledges his life's work as a poet as being part of this universal shamanic quest: "*Dark Movements* is the experience I had trained myself for all these decades. I found myself surrendering to the instinctive extemporaneous and like a dexterous priest or seer, I was able to guide the experience to its utmost capacity for revelation and transformation."

Tim Ingold and Jo Lee Vergunst write in *Ways of Walking* "to follow a trail is to remember how it goes, making one's way in the present is itself a recollection of the past…onward movement is itself a return." For Beam, his pilgrim's progress became about the presentness of his past: "The thrill of the *Dark Movements* collaboration was a return to my very youthful poetry with its origins in Surrealism, Symbolism, and Jung. The distant voices became clearer and clearer telling me to enter the dream, to reveal."

※※※※※※※※

> *…let a work of art act upon us as it acted upon the artist. To grasp its meaning we must allow it to shape us as it shaped him. Then we also understand the nature of his primordial experience. He has*

plunged into the healing and redeeming depths of the collective psyche, where man is not lost in the isolation of consciousness and its errors and suffering, but where all men are caught in common rhythm, which allows the individual to communicate his feelings and strivings to mankind as a whole.
—Carl Jung, *The Spirit in Man, Art and Literature*

Nights through dreams tell the myths forgotten by the day.
—Carl Jung, *Memories, Dreams, Reflections*

✳✳✳✳✳✳✳

Hicks-Jenkins' art is known for its dreamlike quality; Monserrat Pratt, writing in the artist's monograph, describes the original Mari Lwyd series as "more startlingly, deeply oneiric" than anything that had gone before. Dramatising a dark night of the soul, *The Mare's Tale* can be viewed as a secular interpretation of the Stations of the Cross, charting a symbolic journey to the final threshold, where death awaits. The artist completed the first cycle of drawings with a triune Mari, exhausted and broken from a war waged and lost. Father, son, and spectral beast join as one amidst the longest night of a bleak midwinter. There are no scenes of resurrection here.

"I think of an exhibition as being an entire realm of the mind into which the public are invited," commented Hicks-Jenkins, as he prepared to meet the Mari Lwyd once more. "The beast conjured from skull, sheet, and ribbons, which partnered my imagination in a nightmarish Dance of Death, has become infinitely more nuanced to me in the time that has passed." Fifteen years on from the first telling of the story, painter, poet and dancer came together to release dreams from the darkness and to bless the earth with the hope of spring.

Carl Jung, the Swiss psychologist, saw dreams and the imagination as playing an important role in the path to self-knowledge. His hypothesis of the Collective Unconscious proposes that every human being possesses a storehouse of wisdom, common to all religions, peoples and times, of which we are unaware. The Collective Unconscious imparts knowledge through images and symbols, hence the importance of dream interpretation in Jungian depth psychology. Jung believed that artists have the potential to clothe these images and symbols with meaning through their work.

Beam explains, "Learning about Clive's experience of the Mari, I understood the spectral horse of his imaginings had led him on a journey to the primordial source Jung describes in his theories of the psyche, particularly for men." He stated that he found it easy to conjure the gender and color shape-shiftings of Hicks-Jenkins' Mari because of his long-steeped studies—since his undergraduate days—in world myth and folklore, in Jungian archetypes, in the Surrealist subconscious and dreams, and in the Symbolists' and Decadents' phantasmagoria. Even in the larger body of his work—the minimal work alluded to earlier—these notions flow as a subterranean river, there ripe for discovery by perceptive readers adept in their languages.

Spectral Pegasus / Dark Movements begins with the poem *Spectral Pegasus* in which the "Night Mare" manifests in skeletal form, haunting an eerie winter landscape. Out of the subconscious rise the doubts and fears of the ages, before the returning of the light. The "rough and shuffling thing" is not refused entry by the poetic voice; instead, the "Mirror Horse of Heaven" is greeted with the cry: "I eat the night / I welcome it."

The Dark One occurs in many world religions and mythologies, where transformation happens through an encounter with this ancient life force. In his first meeting with Hicks-Jenkins' Mari, it is as if Beam instinctively recognises the shape-shifting animal as his own Pegasus, legendary servant of the poets, who struck a hoof to the sacred earth and a spring of inspiration burst forth. In *The Quickening* an awakening is experienced, as a majestic scarlet horse comes galloping through the cosmic darkness, flowers blooming in its belly, heralding the arrival of new life. Nightmares turn into dreams.

> *We were alone on the hill / when my horse flew through me / Instead of stars my head trilling / with the Lord's passion / Pleasure in the dream // Tranquility of the Holy Thorn! / Tranquility of the Resurrected!*

Seasonal traditions, such as the Mari Lwyd, have long reflected our awe at Nature's annual miracle of death and rebirth. For two gay men, who witnessed a generation of their contemporaries wiped out by the 1980s AIDS epidemic, model/muse Jordan Morley becomes a symbol of a new age dawning and a reminder, lest we forget, of all the promise that was lost. In thanksgiving, painter and poet dip brush and pen in the inky night sky and Morley, re-born as "super natural" man, dances with his horse companion through the dream. In the poem, *The Big Bang: River Jordan:*

> *I am assembling and the wind is blowing / I wear no hat but warm my head with gleam / The prison of my clothes fast disappearing / Into the bat-wing motions wherein I fling // The vastness of my scarf teases my voice / Into a wilderness of wild and tender dances / I bend the wind I turn my forces / I lean and wonder through the Paradise I am*

In *Flowering Skin,* the wind of the spirit carries man and horse into Jung's "world behind the conscious world" and breathes pulsating life into what was once a dance towards death:

> *And you / No skull on stick but majestic / Broken free / A wild beauty / My skin whispers to your springs of Living Water / Flowering earth outshining enemied darkness / And the wounds / the wounds / into April's May have ruby ridden*

Brilliant and disparate elements co-exist in this place of deep dreaming and the images and words, which emerge, linger in the memory, just as on waking it is hard at first to separate ordinary experience from where the mind has traveled to in sleep. Poetry is an act of intense listening. In joining Hicks-Jenkins on his existential pilgrimage, Beam came to the realisation that he was there to tell the story of his own life.

Beam wrote to me, "*Spectral Pegasus / Dark Movements* feels as if I have finally written the myth of my life uttered through kingdoms sacred and profane, mundane and heavenly; through my love of men and sexuality's sublime earthiness; within my psyche's feminine and masculine assemblies; and through my love of Nature and its importance to me as a reservoir and affirmation of the body. It feels so very right and perfect. Even the sounds of the poems express the very hum of my being—which I had never quite perfected before. In my decades of working with the concentrated minimalist poems, I have long had access to my silence, my deep space. But in this book I was thrown back to that young poet who was enthralled by the Universe's noise and cosmic soul-struggle."

Jung viewed the dreamscape as a place of the future, where transformation can happen and potential is explored and unleashed. He documented his own "confrontation with the Unconscious" in words and pictures in *The Red Book* and later urged those he counselled to do the same:

> *I should advise you to put it all down as beautifully as you can… It will seem as if you were making the visions banal—but then you need to do that—then you are freed from the power of them… Then when these things are in some precious book you can go to the book and turn over the pages and for you it will be your church—your cathedral— the silent places of your spirit where you will find renewal. If anyone tells you that it*

is morbid or neurotic and you listen to them—then you will lose your soul—for in that book is your soul.

※※※※※※※※

So I awoke, and behold it was a dream
—John Bunyan, *Pilgrim's Progress*

Your vision will become clear only when you look into your heart… Who looks outside, dreams. Who looks inside, awakens
—C.G. Jung, *Memories, Dreams, Reflections*

Spring has returned. The earth is like a child that knows poems
—Rainer Maria Rilke, *Sonnets to Orpheus: First Series*

※※※※※※※※

Pilgrims walk to change themselves; they walk to find meaning.

Hicks-Jenkins writes of his vocation: "Painting is the shedding of light on things that might otherwise prevent me from sleeping at night. That is pretty much how it is for me, a constant patching-up of some almighty tear in the fabric of heaven with acts of creativity. I suspect it's more common than many might admit to." His poet companion concurs. Beam has long championed the *duende*, rather than the Muse, or Rilke's Angel, as inspirational source. The *duende*, an Iberian quality, which is a combination of "soul" and "fatalism", was made famous by the poet Federico Garcia Lorca. Beam states, "Lorca says, 'The *duende* wounds, and in trying to heal that wound that never heals, lies the strangeness, the inventiveness of a man's work.'" Witness this from the poem "Self-Portrait" in his book *The New Beautiful Tendons: Collected Queer Poems 1969-2012*:

> *A yellow flash / The lamp and my throat shudder // By morning / it has spoken / black and whistling // A strange hand / takes pen // I name you friend*

Pale Horse is a bard's hymn of praise to Nature. The wild song the poet sings is an earth song; the Hallelujah of "super natural" man:

> *Pale man Pale horse beloveds rise / Division's an earthly dreaming / For you have found in wood and flower / The Truth behind all seeming // More This than That more Now than Then / More Yes than No   No Never / Relinquish grief Revive and dance / Your trance welcomes new being*

Ted Hughes described the act of writing poetry as doing "one thing" which is "to imagine what you are writing about… Just look at it, touch it, smell it, listen to it, turn yourself into it… So you keep going as long as you can, then look back and see what you have written… and you will get a shock. You will have captured a spirit, a creature." *Meeting the Centaur: Horse/Man* is such a *fiat* of the poet's imagination—a Divine Being manifesting in all its radiance:

> *I am the Dark One all more beautiful / I germinate and shepherd within the Green / And Blue my talisman to my dying self / And horse myself into reviving God*

In this poem, Beam pays homage to Rainer Maria Rilke's *Widening Circles* and, in doing so, finds himself walking alongside the pilgrim souls of his poet ancestors, who made it their mission to seek out their own unique spiritual path:

At the end of the poem, the numinous Horse/Man, the progeny of the *Dark Movements* creative union, is left by poet and painter to reign supreme in the Otherworld, while the common man returns to his earthly home, infused with new passion and power and the knowledge that all must die to grow.

As the *Dark Movements* exhibition launched in June 2015, the United States Supreme Court ruled that state-level bans on same-sex marriage are unconstitutional. Beam and Stanley Finch married in November 2014 and had their union blessed in church six months later, a week before the couple's 35th anniversary. The poet, whose life's work has been to root his body in a deified sexuality—Nature in Spirit—writes in his essay *The Visionary Company of Love*: "Grace resides within each of us, whomever we love. I don't require that you become as I am. But if you require, as the great teachers have, that 'I know myself,' you must accept who I am."

The pilgrimage ends at the beginning with the painting and poem *Birth,* and the in-between place is glimpsed where opposites are experienced as one. In this realm of transformation, the Mari's shroud becomes a man's marriage veil:

In *Spectral Pegasus / Dark Movements*, the painter and the poet have forged into one the old and a new Hero's mythic journey. The grace of these paintings and poems is in their very wildness, their Queer passage in which the fluidity of gender, of divine being, of the veils between death and life, innocence and experience, thrust the two pilgrims into the darkness and then a coming through—an embrace of the unknown and the unknowable. This is William Blake's eternal bliss, his "eternity in an hour" confessed through the shroud of the Mari Lwyd.

Sarah Parvin, The Curious One
December 2016
Leeds, Yorkshire, England

REFERENCES

Eliade, Mircea. *Shamanism: Archaic Techniques of Ecstasy*, Princeton, NJ: Princeton University Press, 1964

Ingold, Tim, (Editor) and Lee, Jo, (Editor). *Ways of Walking: Ethnography and Practice on Foot* (Anthropological Studies of Creativity and Perception), New York: Routledge, 2008

Clive Hicks-Jenkins, London: Lund Humphries, 2011

Corbett, Sara. *Holy Grail of the Unconscious*, *New York Times Magazine*, Sept. 16, 2009

Driscoll, Chad. www.oysterboyreview.org/issue/12/DriscollC-EditorsNote.html

Jung, Carl G. *Memories, Dreams, Reflections*, London: Fontana Press, 2001

Jung, Carl G. *The Spirit in Man, Art and Literature*, London; New York: Routledge, 2001

Hughes, Ted. *Poetry in the Making*, London: Faber and Faber, 1967

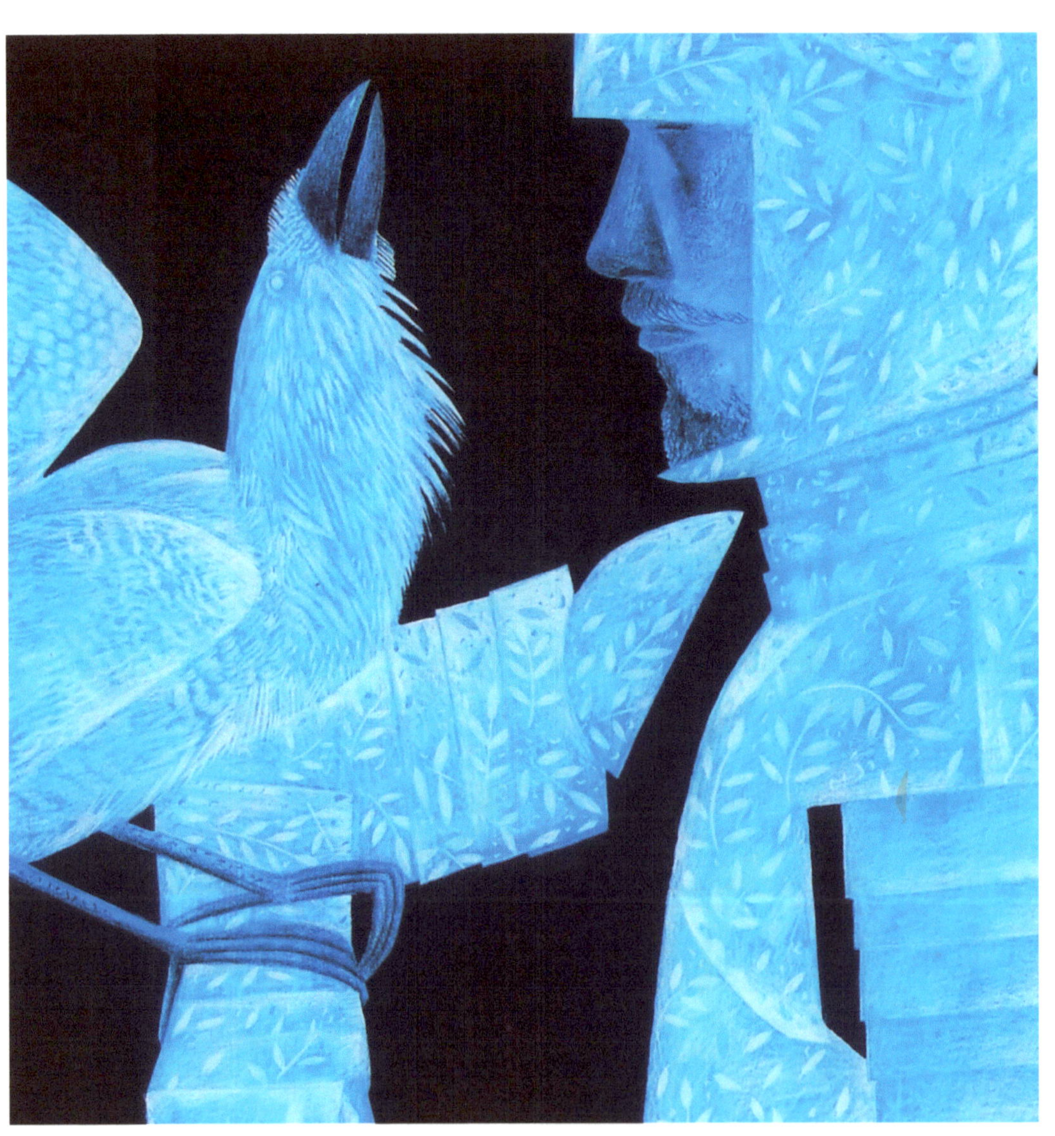

DARK MOVEMENTS: CLIVE HICKS-JENKINS AND THE RETURN OF THE MARI LWYD

So many things are meeting in these new works: my original drawings for the Mare's Tale (and my family history that underlies them) the recent collaborations with my model, Jordan Morley, themes of greening and renewal, my love and use of toy theatre in my practice, and of course, that old discipline of mine, long behind me but always present in my mind…and in muscle-memory…the dance.
—Clive Hicks-Jenkins, *Artlog*

Tra yr ystyriwyf lawer o chwareuon ac ymdrechfeydd corfforol nid yn unig yn ddiniwed, ond yn llesiol i'r ieuenctyd; eto, meddwl yr wyf y dylid anghefnogi a gwrthwynebu pob chwareuaeth, a phob arferiad traddodiadol arall, sydd yn tarddu oddiwrth goelgrefydd a Phabyddiaeth, fel pethau sydd yn ymyraeth yn niweidiol â'r meddwl ieuanc.

While I do consider many games and physical activities to be not only innocent but beneficial to youth, I nonetheless think it best to reject and oppose all manner of games and other traditions which have their origins in superstition and Popery, as things which have a harmful effect on the youthful mind.
—William Roberts, 1852

※※※※※※※※

The horse has returned. A new cycle, new images; renewed meanings. The return is both insistent and revelatory, which is pretty much as it should be. It is the nature of the beast.

In 1852 William Roberts ('Nefydd'), a Baptist minister from Blaenau Gwent, Wales, published *Crefydd yr Oesoedd Tywyll: neu Henafiaethau Defodol, Chwareu-yddol, a Choelgrefyddol* (*The Religion of the Dark Ages: or Rituals, Games and Superstitions of Antiquity*), a composite collection containing a prizewinning *eisteddfod** essay on the Mari Lwyd. It's a fascinating read, especially the preface. Starting from the unshakeable premise that the only good tradition is a dead tradition, Roberts twists and turns around his material with a discomfort bordering on self-hate. Furious as hell that people might think for one moment that he is *interested* in this stuff, he fences it off with footnotes and buries it deep under learning. Locating the roots of the tradition in a Roman past gives them a patina of Classical respectability, and signals that they are very, very dead.

It is always a mistake, however, to tell people in anything but the vaguest terms what they shouldn't be doing. Nothing is racier, weirder, or more perverse than a book of medieval *exempla*: little stories of *thou shalt nots* held up by the Church (read Chapel) for us all to shiver in fear, in excitement. When Roberts included in his essay twenty verses from the traditional Mari Lwyd mumming dialogue he probably thought of them as a threnody. But it was also an act of salvage. Mere proclamation of her death was excuse enough: the bones were up and rattling off down lanes, past pubs, through the cobbled streets of seaside towns. By now a necessary part of the corpus of traditional (revived/renewed/preserved) Welsh folk practices, the Mari comes in various guises (including, for those without easy access to horses' skulls, a stylish cardboard flat-pack version: Mari Lwyd meets IKEA). She stalks, too, through Welsh literature, ghosting the self-loathing of Caradoc Evans and "ripping the stitch of grief" in Vernon Watkins' wartime *Ballad of the Mari Lwyd*. More recently, she can be found in the psychogeographical wanderings of Iain Sinclair's *Black Apples of Gower*, and giving form to a childhood terror in Francesca Rhydderch's novel *The Rice Paper Diaries*.

For nearly two decades the horse's skull, the white sheets, and the ambiguous twisting bodies have haunted the work of the Welsh artist Clive Hicks-Jenkins. The earlier incarnations were discussed with great insight by Monserrat Prat in the monograph *Clive Hicks-Jenkins*, who reads in the sequence of Mari Lwyd works developed between 1998 and 2002 a double skein of loss and fear. The aftershocks of a society blighted by AIDS (which took an especially cruel toll on the theatre world, where Hicks-Jenkins had his first career) combine with the intensely personal story of his dying father, tormented at the end of his life by a traumatic childhood encounter with the Monmouthshire Mari. Since then there have been further visitations, including *The Mare's Tale*, a striking stage production which (and this is typical of the collaborative, multi-dimensional nature of the artist's work) combined puppetry and film with a libretto by the poet Welsh poet Damian Walford Davies and a score by Mark Bowden. This work, performed in Theatr Brycheiniog in 2013, drew on an earlier sequence of poems and drawings also called *The Mare's Tale*, published by the Old Stile Press in 2001. The early death of that first collaborator, the Welsh poet Catriona Urquhart, poignantly informed the stage-play's narrative of loss.

Many of these elements were reconfigured when Aberystwyth Arts Centre in Aberystwyth, Wales hosted a new phase of the work, *Dark Movements,* in June 2015. As ever, this was a dynamic, collaborative affair. Alongside some of Urquhart's original poems were extracts from the collection *Spectral Pegasus / Dark Movements* by American poet Jeffery Beam, and an actual toy theatre (and anyone with an inkling of the Hicks-Jenkins' take on 'toys' will know straight away that this should induce a frisson of something akin to fear). English composer Peter Byrom Smith provided a soundtrack, both for the exhibition and for a film deriving from the work, directed by fellow Welshman Pete Telfer. The sets designed for the toy theatre are especially beautiful things: the great white skeletal horse arcs over a strange out-of-kilter village washed in bluewhite moonlight, where connoisseurs of the paintings will spot those familiar Hicks-Jenkins landmarks, the viaduct and the tower.

But the dominant note of this work is a surprising one. A new artistic partnership with the American performance artist Jordan Morley and poet Beam has produced a new Mari Lwyd. Where the earlier sequence of drawings and etchings moved principally in themes of light and dark—black, bone-white, grey—the keynotes of this Mari have an oriental intensity, all reds and blues; these are trademark Hicks-Jenkins colours, but they are unexpected here. In *The Quickening*, complex leafy branchings with curious cog-like flowers burst from the horse's ribcage; tendrils spill out, exploratory, alive. The erotic proximities of man and beast are intriguing and unnerving; there is a tenderness here which recalls the *Hervé and the Wolf* sequence—but the blood-red horse's head, though less skull-like than earlier versions, is rigid and flayed. The male figure lies in strange poses derived from the artist's use of maquettes (again, a reference to the puppet world of the toy theatre), twisting the supple dancer's limbs into ever more unnatural positions. The use of maquettes is another distinctive feature of the Hicks-Jenkins oeuvre, a distancing technique he says he developed to overcome the perennial problem (admit it, we've all been there) of how to depict the wings of angels.

Anxiety about authenticity is the bane of folk world, and it is always a relief to come across a fiercely personal artistic vision that can chew up the raw materials of tradition and spit them out so energetically. It's a pity that the word 'channelled' is currently overused and thus unusable, because that's exactly what is happening here: 'channelling' properly captures the balance between controlling and yielding. Between the rider, and the ridden. No coincidence that William Roberts should write, a trifle helplessly, of the need to *resist* tradition: *meddwl yr wyf ei bod yn bryd gwrthsefyll y ffrwd hyd ag y mae ynom* ("I think it is time to resist the [*ffrwd*] as far as we are able"). *Ffrwd* could be decorously translated as 'influence' here, but it has the force of a torrent, a rushing mountain stream.

The sign of a 'real' tradition must be its irreducibility to a single discourse or a single dimension: it cannot be explained, not permanently. But you know you're on to something when the shapes of such a tradition fit the events of real life (the story of a father's death, for example), without losing their alien quality of myth. The narrative/visual atoms cluster and regroup in ways that are instantly recognizable and recognizably different. Hence this work's subliminal affinity with Robert Graves's similarly vivid, non-metaphorical, post-WW1 vision of the Night-Mare:

Her nests, when one comes across them in dreams, lodged in rock-clefts or the branches of enormous hollow yews, are built of carefully chosen twigs, lined with white horse-hair and the plumage of prophetic birds and littered with the jaw bones and entrails of poets. The prophet Job said of her: "She dwelleth and abideth on the rock. Her young ones also suck up blood."

*The *eisteddfod* is a Welsh festival of literature, music and performance. The tradition of such a meeting of Welsh artists dates back to at least the 12th century.

Mary-Ann Constantine

REFERENCES

www.hicksjenkins.com

William Roberts (Nefydd), *Crefydd yr Oesoedd Tywyll, neu Henafiaethau Defodol, Chwareu-yddol, a Choelgrefyddol* (Caerfyrddin, 1852)

Monserrat Prat, "Metamorphosis of a Folk Tradition" in *Clive Hicks-Jenkins* (Farnham: Lund Humphries, 2011) 62-79

For the traditional practices of the Mari Lwyd (including the flat-pack incarnation) see
www.trac-cymru.org/en/projects/mari-lwyd

A NOTE ON
CLIVE HICKS-JENKINS' *DARK MOVEMENTS*

The foundation of this exhibition is the series of drawings entitled *The Mare's Tale* produced by Clive Hicks-Jenkins in the early years of this century and shortly after the death of his father, Trevor. Throughout his life, Trevor Jenkins was haunted by the Welsh tradition of the Mari Lwyd — the figure composed of sheet, ribbon, bells, and horse's skull that is carried from door to door at New Year. The drawings produced by the son depict the final illness of the father; the figure of the Mari Lwyd is present throughout, both exemplifying and intensifying the emotions of grief and loss that the artist explores.

As Hicks-Jenkins explains in his notes to the exhibition, he assumed that when he finished *The Mare's Tale*, he had concluded his artistic involvement with the Mari Lwyd. However, over the past couple of years, Hicks-Jenkins has produced a new series of paintings that revisit the legend. These paintings stand alongside the earlier works and in some ways provide a counterpart to them. The earlier monochrome, lightened by only occasional hints of colour, gives way to an explosion of blood red and rich blue. The sculptural quality of the figures in the drawings is replaced by the disjointed marionette-style forms of the paintings.

These two series provide the apparent starting and closing points of *Dark Movements*. Yet, to see the work in this exhibition simply as part of a linear progression is to overlook one of its most striking features — its profoundly collaborative nature. Hicks-Jenkins' work is accompanied by poems by Jeffery Beam and the late Catriona Urquhart, herself a friend of Trevor Jenkins. Designs for a collaborative musical piece, created with Mark Bowden and Damian Walford Davies, stand alongside a film by Pete Telfer, itself accompanied by music by Peter Byrom-Smith. [In 2001 The Old Stile Press had published *The Mare's Tale* illustrated by Hicks-Jenkins, a sequence of poems Catriona had written examining Hicks-Jenkins' father's early experience of the Welsh Mari Lwyd mumming tradition.]

In his notes and on his website, Hicks-Jenkins has traced the various ways in which such collaborations came into being. He emphasizes the genuinely mutual nature of these creative processes. The accompanying pieces are not simply commentaries upon Hicks-Jenkins' work; they are independent creations that have, in turn, prompted further interventions from the artist. Indeed, the entire impetus for *Dark Movements* came from the unanticipated reaction of American dancer, Jordan Morley, to Hicks-Jenkins' exploration of the Mari Lwyd tradition. In response to Hicks-Jenkins' original drawings of the dancer, Morley independently photographed himself in poses inspired by the drawings of *The Mare's Tale* series. Hicks-Jenkins built maquettes based upon these photographs, which in turn led to the paintings of the series. These paintings prompted the creation of poems by Beam which in turn prompted further paintings by Hicks-Jenkins.

Walking through the exhibition, it is impossible not to be aware of these cross currents. The landscape of the Borderlands series, simultaneously deeply Welsh and almost lunar in its strangeness, is echoed and reimagined in both film and poem. Poems speak to each other — Beam's *Spectral Pegasus*, written during the creation of the Dark Movements Toy Theatre, communicates with Urquhart's poem *Pegasus* whilst also standing in dialogue with Hicks-Jenkins' painting of the same name. Our awareness of Urquhart's early death adds a further layer of sadness to her elegiac poem's position within *The Mare's Tale* series.

Such connections can be tracked in seemingly endless ways across the exhibition. This is both fascinating and disturbing. The echoes reflect the nature of the Mari Lwyd tradition itself, expressive of the constant turning and returning of the years. They also contribute to our sense that the individual works within the exhibition — so rich in themselves — become richer still as part of a greater whole. As Hicks-Jenkins writes, "Collaborations, when they work well, fly back and forth between the participants with increasing energy." These collaborations work profoundly well, enhancing both one another and their mutual attempt to understand the tradition of the Mari Lwyd. The energy created through their connections helps to counter the darker movements indicated in the exhibition's title.

Claire Pickard

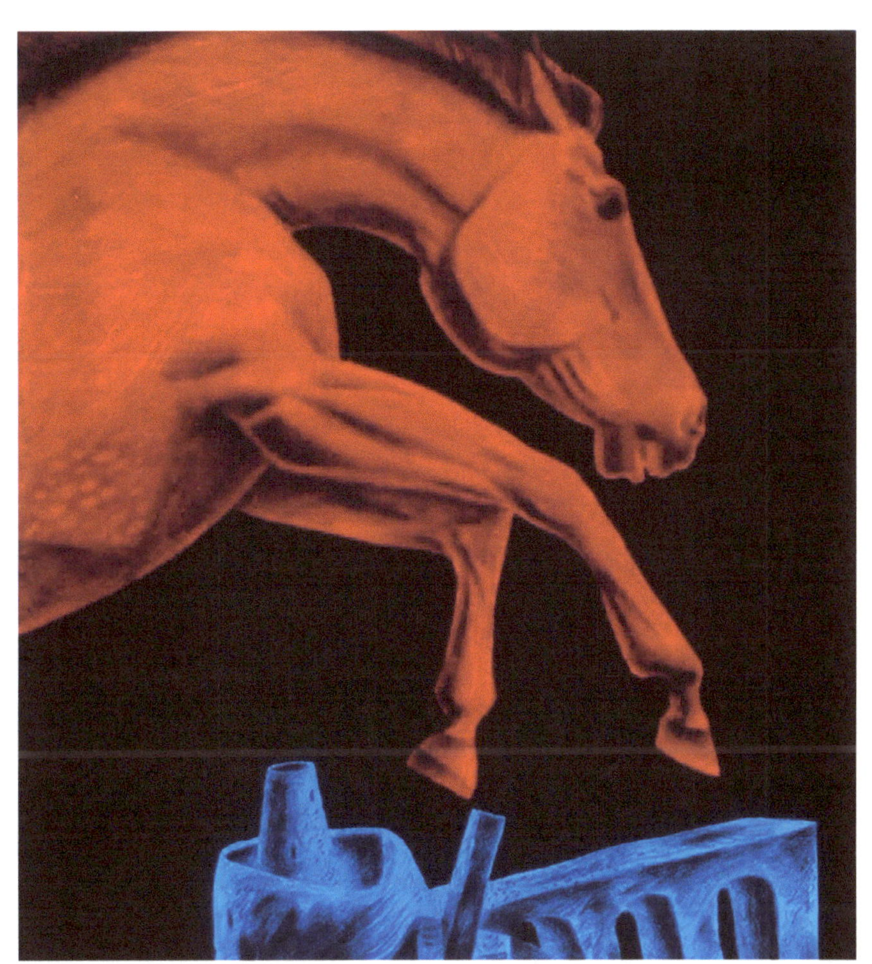

Jeffery Beam's many award-winning works include *The Broken Flower* (Skysill Press, England), *Gospel Earth* (Skysill Press, England), *Visions of Dame Kind* (The Jargon Society), *An Elizabethan Bestiary: Retold* (Horse & Buggy), *The New Beautiful Tendons: Collected Queer Poems 1969–2012* (Spuyten Duyvil-Triton), *Light and Shadow* (Aperture), and *The Fountain* (NC Wesleyan College Press). His spoken word CD with multimedia *What We Have Lost: New and Selected Poems 1977-2001* was a 2003 Audio Publishers Award finalist. Beam's latest works are *Jonathan Williams: The Lord of Orchards* (co-edited with Richard Owens, Prospecta Press, 2018), and a virtual chapbook *Don't Forget Love* (*Dispatches from the Poetry Wars*, 2018, dispatchespoetrywars.com/virtual-chapbooks/2018/04/ dont-forget-love-by-jeffrey-beam). The song cycle, *Life of the Bee* (composer Lee Hoiby) continues to be performed on the international stage and can be heard, along with a Beam reading of the texts, on Albany Record's *New Growth*, a recording of the Carnegie Hall premiere. Limited fine editions include *An Invocation* (Country Valley Press), *On Hounded Ground: Home and the Creative Life* (Bookgirl Press, Japan), *MountSeaEden* (Chester Creek Press), and *Eno Crow* (Horse & Buggy Press). A number of young composers have worked and are working with his poetry. Steven Serpa premiered the cantata *Heaven's Birds: Lament and Song* (based on three *New Beautiful Tendons* poems) on Boston's World AIDS Day 2008. His tone poem *An Invocation* premiered for string quartet in 2014 (Spartanburg, SC) and in 2016 as a symphonic piece (Austin Symphony). Serpa premiered *The Creatures: A Bestiary Retold* (Austin, 2016) and also plans a song cycle of gay love poems. Holt McCarley premiered an instrumental piece, *The Hyena*, from the *Bestiary* (St. Louis, 2015) and is working on two cycles based on Beam nature and love poems. 2015 also saw the premier of a Daniel Thomas Davis chamber opera *Kith & Kin: Seven Portraits* with song texts by several North Carolina writers, including Beam (restaged with North Carolina Opera premier in 2018). Tony Solitro's song *Love's Astronomy* was completed in August 2018 and by the time of this printing will have had its first performance. Forthcoming is Beam's first of several projected children's books *The Droods* with British artist Phil Cooper. Other projects include *Bee, I'm Expecting You* (bee poem anthology), and *Blue Darter - Jonathan Williams: A Bibliography of the Publications and Ephemera, 1950–2008*. He continues to work on the poetry collection *Life of the Bee; Bee, I'm Expecting You*—an anthology of bee poems, facts, and folklore through the ages; and *They Say: A Commonplace Book on Poetry and the Spirit*. Beam's poems and criticism have appeared in many anthologies and magazines. Poetry editor emeritus of the print and online literary journal *Oyster Boy Review*, Beam retired in late 2011 from many decades as a UNC-Chapel Hill botanical librarian. Born in Kannapolis, North Carolina he lives in Hillsborough with his husband of 39 years, Stanley Finch. You can learn more about, read and hear more of his poetry at his website: www.jefferybeam.com

In **Clive Hicks-Jenkins**' early career he was an actor, choreographer, director, and stage designer, creating productions with leading companies in London. He moved back to Wales permanently in the late 1980's to concentrate on his work as an artist. The actor Simon Callow has called him "one of the most individual and complete artists of our time" and Nicholas Usherwood in Galleries has described his work as "reflective, expressive painting of the highest order." His paintings, prints and artists' books are in numerous public collections, including the National Museum of Wales, the Glynn Vivian Art Gallery, the Museum of Modern Art Machynlleth, the Contemporary Art Society for Wales, Llandaff Cathedral, Pallant House Gallery, and the Methodist Church Collection of Modern Art, as well as private collections around the world. His artist's books, including the first illustrated edition of Peter Shaffer's *Equus*, are in libraries worldwide. Clive was winner of the Gulbenkian Welsh Art Prize in 1999, runner-up as Welsh Artist of the Year in April 2000, and in 2002 received a Creative Wales Award from the Arts Council of Wales. He is a Royal Cambrian Academician and an Honorary Fellow of Aberystwyth University School of Art. He has had solo exhibitions at Martin Tinney Gallery, Newport Museum & Art Gallery, Brecknock Museum, the Museum of Modern Art Wales, and Christ Church Picture Gallery in Oxford. In 2011, his work was celebrated in a hugely successful retrospective at the National Library of Wales, Aberystwyth. His latest exhibition featured a limited edition series of 14 screenprints, and supplemental paintings and drawings, on the theme Sir Gawain and the Green Knight. These screenprints have been reproduced in a new edition of Simon Armitage's translation of the poem (Faber & Faber, 2018) which served as inspiration for the series. 2016 saw the publication of his first illustrated book *Hansel and Gretel* (Random Spectacular). In 2018 Goldfield Productions' *Hansel and Gretel: A Nightmare in Eight Scenes*, inspired by Clive's images and under his direction and design supervision, toured England to great acclaim. [Composer Matthew Kaner, poet Simon Armitage, and a team of visual and puppetry artists.] Armitage's retelling of the tale with Clive's illustrations was published by Design For Today in the autumn of 2018. In Spring 2019, the Berkley Ensemble will be presenting the first public concert performances of *The Mare's Tale* by composer Mark Bowden and librettist poet Damian Walford Davies, across England, Wales and Scotland. Clive-Jenkins has been praised by critics in *The Independent, Modern Painters, Art Review, Galleries, The New Welsh Review, Planet,* and the BBC Wales series *Double Yellow.* His work has also been selected for several prestigious group exhibitions, including the Royal Academy. *The Book of Ystwyth: Six Poets on the Art of Clive Hicks-Jenkins* (Carolina Wren Press) and the noteworthy monograph *Clive Hicks-Jenkins* (Lund Humphries) were both published by in 2011. www.hicks-jenkins.com AND clivehicksjenkins.wordpress.com

Mary-Ann Constantine studies Romantic period literature, with an emphasis on Wales and Brittany, at the University of Wales Centre for Advanced Welsh and Celtic Studies in Aberystwyth and has published widely in these fields since 1996. Her short stories have appeared over a number of years in the *New Welsh Review* and *Planet* and her first collection, *The Breathing,* was published by *Planet* in 2008. Her second collection, *All the Souls,* was published by Seren in spring 2013. She is the author of the novel *Star-Shot* (Seren, 2016) and a number of scholarly works.

Sarah Parvin (a.k.a. The Curious One) is a wearer of several hats, all of them linked to a common theme—an innate desire to know more. Sarah lives in Yorkshire and works as a freelance marketing, branding, and trend forecasting consultant. She is also trained in Cognitive Behavioural Therapy and Jungian Psychological Astrology. Sarah created *The Curious One,* which boasts a Pinterest following of 275k, as a vehicle to explore the British imagination, through the work of its artists, illustrators, makers, poets, writers, photographers, and designers. She enjoys using her wide-ranging experience to help creatives of every calling turn their labours of love into sustainable realities. www.thecuriousone.com

Claire Pickard writes for *New Welsh Review.*

Mary Rocap has been singing and playing music in the Piedmont of North Carolina since the mid-70s. Her song writing is influenced by the folk streams of Southern gospel, particularly Sacred Harp and spirituals, traditional ballads, and the blues. She has released four CDs of original work and one CD of gospel songs. She also bakes, quilts, and chronicles the escapades and calamities of her backyard flock of chickens. www.maryrocap.com

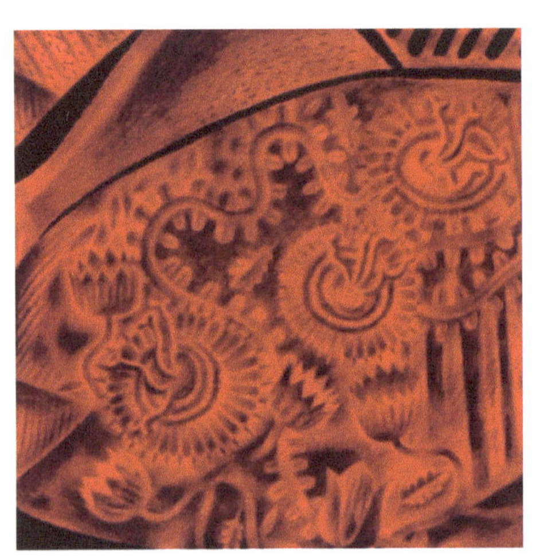

SPECTRAL PEGASUS / DARK MOVEMENTS

Published by Kin Press
Design, layout and editing by J.C. Mlozanowski
Cover design by J.C. Mlozanowski

This book was built using Adobe Creative Cloud. Titles are rendered in Maiandra GD, a typeface inspired by the hand-lettering of artist-designer Oswald Bruce Cooper and influenced by Greek epigraphy. Poems are presented in Constantia, a serif font influenced by the Perpetua typeface designed by English sculptor-stonemason Eric Gill. Essays and other text are presented in Palatino Linotype, designed by calligrapher-designer Hermann Zapf and named after Italian calligrapher Giambattista Palatino.

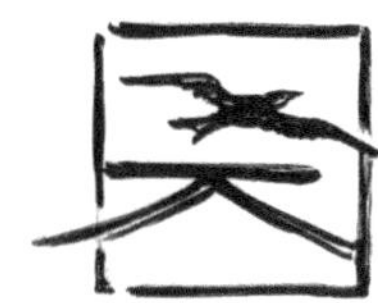